An Introduction to Picture Collecting

An Introduction to Picture Collecting

Peter Mitchell

Arthur Barker Limited
5 Winsley Street London W1

First Published September 1968

Second impression December 1968

SBN 213 76324 9

Made and Printed in Great Britain by C. Tinling & Co. Ltd.
Liverpool, London and Prescot

Acknowledgements

I am grateful to my father for his helpful interest in the preparation of this book. Miss Charlotte Prest of Sotheby & Company, and Miss Angelina Morhange of Christie's have been especially kind in helping me with the sales records of their respective firms. My thanks are also due to our secretary, Mr P. Malcolm Uttley, for his careful typing of the manuscript. Lastly, I hope that I have acknowledged in the appropriate places the information I have quoted from the work of different authors.

February 1968 P. J. M.

Contents

List of Illustrations viii

Introduction xiii

1 Of Blisters, Buttons, Keys and Scumble: Pictures as Physical Objects 1

2 More Looking and Learning 38

3 How to Buy 56

4 What to Buy 73

5 Investment and the Care of Paintings 117

Index 123

List of Illustrations

1 Detail from 'A View of Amsterdam' by ABRAHAM STORCK (1635-1710), showing characteristic seventeenth-century *craquelure*

2 Detail from a painting by JULIUS CAESAR IBBETSON (1759-1817), showing characteristic eighteenth-century *craquelure* and use of impasto

The Eighteenth Century
Marines

3 WILLIAM ANDERSON (1757-1837)
'The Thames at Rotherhithe'
Watercolour
Signed and dated 1790
Size: 8¼ × 10½ inches

4 JOHN CLEVELEY JNR (1747-86)
'Torre de San Vicente de Belem, on the River Tagus, Lisbon'
Watercolour
Signed and dated 1778
Size: 18 × 24 inches
Described and illustrated in colour in *Sea Painters of Britain* by F. G. Roe, plate 4 (F. Lewis, 1947)

5 NICHOLAS POCOCK (1741-1821)
'Launching a fishing boat'
Watercolour, oval
Signed and dated 1789
Size: 10½ × 14½ inches

6 HENRY MOSES (*c*.1779-1860)
'Men-o'-War off Eddystone'
Watercolour, oval
Signed and dated 14 January 1797
Size: 6¾ × 8½ inches
Lit: *A Dictionary of British Marine Painters*, by Arnold Wilson

7 HENRY MOSES
'Marine view'
Watercolour, oval
Signed and dated 10 January 1797
Size: 6¾ × 8½ inches
Lit: *A Dictionary of British Marine Painters*, by Arnold Wilson

8 JOHN THOMAS SERRES (1759-1825) 'A View of Leghorn'
Oil on canvas
Signed and dated 1799, and inscribed 'Livorno'
Size: 15¼ × 24 inches

9 THOMAS LUNY (1758-1837)
'Shipping in Southampton Water'
Oil on canvas
Signed and dated 1788
Size: 21¾ × 33¾ inches

Landscapes

10 GEORGE SMITH OF CHICHESTER (1714-76)
'The First Premium landscape painting of 1760, with portraits of the three Smith of Chichester brothers'
Oil on canvas
Size: 30½ × 38½ inches

11 GEORGE & JOHN SMITH OF CHICHESTER
'Returning from Market'
Oil on canvas
Signed
Size: 12 × 17 inches

12 GEORGE SMITH OF CHICHESTER
'Winter Landscape'
Oil on canvas
Signed
Size: 12½ × 17 inches

13 THOMAS JONES (*c*.1730-1803)
'Landscape with figures and a Boat on a Lake'
Oil on canvas
Signed
Size: 19 × 24 inches

14 JOSEPH FARINGTON (1747-1821)
'Basildon Church and Friary from Streatley Hill, Berks.'
Watercolour
Signed and dated 1792
Size: 8½ × 11⅞ inches

15 SAMUEL H. GRIMM (1734-94)
'Shire Green and Grenoside, Yorkshire'
Watercolour
Signed and dated 1781
Size: 15 × 21 inches

16 WILLIAM PAYNE (1760-1815)
'Weymouth and Portland'
Watercolour
Signed
Size: 11¾ × 16 inches

17 MOSES GRIFFITH (1749-*c*.1810)
'Llanbedr Hall, Denbighshire, 1805'
Watercolour
Signed and dated 1 August 1805, and inscribed on reverse
Size: 11½ × 15½ inches

18 PETER LA CAVE (worked 1769-1810)
'Landscape with Figures and Watermill'
Watercolour
Signed and dated 1801
Size: 7¼ × 9¾ inches

19 FRANCIS NICHOLSON (1753-1844)
'Loch Lomond'
Watercolour
Signed and dated 1794 on mount, inscribed on reverse
Size: 11¾ × 16¼ inches

20 FRANCIS NICHOLSON
'The Grass Market, Edinburgh'
Watercolour
Signed and dated 1807, and in-

scribed on reverse: 'From the corner of the Grass Market, Edinburgh, F. Nicholson 1807'
Size: 14½ × 20 inches
Coll: Wathan. H. Lee Warner, Riberton Court 1828
Exhib: Old Watercolour Society 1807, No. 315

21 DOMINIC SERRES (1722-93)
'Landscape with a Cottage beside a Wood'
Oil on canvas
Signed and dated 1762
Size: 12 × 14 inches

22 JULIUS CAESAR IBBETSON (1759-1817)
'A View of Kilburn with London and St Paul's in the Distance'
Watercolour
Signed and dated 1787, and inscribed 'Kilburn'
Size: 10½ × 13 inches

23 JULIUS CAESAR IBBETSON
'A View of Kilburn with London in the Distance'
Watercolour
Signed and dated 1787, and inscribed 'Kilburn'
Size: 10½ × 13 inches

24 JULIUS CAESAR IBBETSON
'A View of Harrow from Kilburn'
Oil on canvas
Signed, inscribed and dated 1787
Size: 20 × 26 inches
Exhib: Royal Academy, London, 1787, No. 142
Exhibition of British Art, Royal Academy, 1934, No. 577
Growth of London Exhibition, Victoria & Albert Museum, 1964
Lit: R. Mary Clay, *Julius Caesar Ibbetson*, page 14

25 PAUL SANDBY, RA (1725-1809)
'Gathering Fuel in Windsor Great Park'
Watercolour
Size: 9½ × 12 inches

26 PAUL SANDY, RA
'View of Cory-lin on the Upper Clyde'
Gouache
Signed
Size: 12½ × 17½ inches

27 PAUL SANDBY, RA
'Pembroke Castle from the West'
Oil on panel
Inscribed on reverse
Size: 12 × 18¾ inches
Exhib: Royal Academy 1808, No. 565

28 THOMAS ROWLANDSON (1756-1827)
'Travellers on Bodmin Moor'
Watercolour, pen and ink
Size: 6¾ × 9½ inches

29 CHARLES TOWNE (1763-1840)
'Landscape with Figures, Horses and Sheep'
Oil on canvas
Signed with monogram
Size: 24 × 31½ inches

30 JOHN SELL COTMAN (1782-1842)
'Leatherhead Church'
Watercolour
Signed and dated 1800, and inscribed on reverse
Size: $14\frac{1}{4} \times 21$ inches
Exhib: Royal Academy 1800, No. 424

31 JOHN CONSTABLE (1776-1837)
'At Buckden, Yorks.'
Watercolour
Inscribed and dated 1832
Size: $5\frac{7}{8} \times 8\frac{3}{4}$ inches

Portraiture

32 JOHN RUSSELL (1744-1806)
'Portrait of a Young Girl in a Red Cloak'
Pastel
Size: $21\frac{1}{2} \times 15\frac{1}{2}$ inches

33 SIR MARTIN ARCHER SHEE (1769-1850)
'Portrait of Captain Edward Becher'
Oil on canvas
Size: 30×25 inches

34 JOHN DOWNMAN, RA (1750-1824)
'Portrait of Mrs Mary Seawell of Great Bookham'
Watercolour, oval
Signed and dated 1792
Size: $8 \times 6\frac{3}{4}$ inches

The Nineteenth Century

35 GEORGE CHAMBERS (1803-40)
'Bleak House, Broadstairs'
Oil on artist's millboard
Signed
Size: 11×18 inches

36 JAMES HOLLAND (1800-1870)
'A View of Margate'
Watercolour
Inscribed and dated 23 September 1861
Size: 4×6 inches

37 JAMES BAKER PYNE (1800-1870)
'The Post-town of Luino, Lago Maggiore'
Oil on canvas
Signed and dated 1869, and numbered No. 726
Size: $26\frac{1}{4} \times 39\frac{1}{2}$ inches

38 JAMES WILSON CARMICHAEL (1800-1868)
'Shipping off Portsmouth'
Oil on canvas
Signed and dated 1863
Size: 24×39 inches

39 JAMES WILSON CARMICHAEL
'A View of Durham'
Oil on artist's millboard
Signed
Size: 9×13 inches

40 DAVID ROBERTS, RA (1796-1864)
'The Priory of Pluscardine, Morayshire'
Watercolour
Signed, inscribed and dated 12 September 1848
Size: $9\frac{1}{2} \times 13\frac{1}{2}$ inches

Other Schools

41 FRANCESCO FERNANDI called IMPERIALI (1679-1741)

'The Contest of Apollo and Marsyas'
Oil on canvas
Size: $20\frac{1}{4} \times 25\frac{3}{4}$ inches

42 HENRI - JOSEPH HARPIGNIES (1819-1916)
'A View in Lombardy'
Watercolour
Signed and dated 1861
Size: $9\frac{1}{2} \times 16\frac{1}{2}$ inches

43 BERNARDUS-JOHANNES BLOMMERS (1845-1914)
'Beach Scene'
Oil on canvas laid down on board
Signed
Size: $4\frac{3}{4} \times 7\frac{1}{4}$ inches

44 JEAN - LÉON GÉRÔME (1824-1904)
'A View of Jerusalem'
Oil on canvas
Signed and inscribed
Size: $8\frac{3}{4} \times 12$ inches

45 JEAN-LÉON GÉRÔME
'A View of Baalbek'
Oil on canvas
Signed and inscribed
Size: $8\frac{3}{4} \times 12$ inches

46 MAURICE COURANT (1847-1925)
'Beach Scene'
Oil on canvas
Signed and dated 1906
Size: $18\frac{3}{8} \times 15$ inches

47 PIETER WITHOOS (1654-93)
'A Garden Tulip'
Gouache
Signed and dated 1683
Size: $12\frac{5}{8} \times 8$ inches

48 PIETER WITHOOS
'A Garden Tulip'
Gouache
Signed and dated 1683
Size: $12\frac{5}{8} \times 8$ inches

Photography by A. C. Cooper Ltd, 10 Pollen Street, London W1

Introduction

Everyone is a collector at heart. The collecting urge is deeply rooted and finds an outlet in everything from paperweights to model steam engines. One form of collecting has always held pride of place – picture collecting. The joys of picture collecting are too long established and too well-known to need enumeration. Indeed, more and more people are aware of them, and the impetus given to picture collecting today has many causes. At the root is the simple realization that the pursuit of material prosperity, however successful, may leave a kind of aesthetic void in our lives. Yet the very prosperity which tends to push aside such considerations can provide the means and the time to fulfil them.

You may feel that 'collector' is rather a pretentious word for the modest buyer of paintings, and it is true that most people hesitate to use the word about themselves. In the same way, they will buy a picture because a space in the hall needs filling, rather than feeling anything of the 'void' I have mentioned. Whatever your motives for buying pictures, and on whatever scale you intend doing so, this guide is written to give you help and encouragement – but never false encouragement. It is not a teach-yourself book, which if diligently pursued to the end will ensure complete mastery of the subject. If this were so, picture collecting would be too easy and its great rewards too readily attained. Rather does this guide offer pointers towards the right approach and the knowledge which will be needed – knowledge of theory allied and interwoven with practical know-how. Successful collecting will in the end depend on an individual's taste, eye and knowledge. To discover how far you possess these attributes, and to allow them to develop, you must give yourself the opportunity and never underrate yourself until you have done so. My object in this short guide is to help you to give yourself that opportunity.

Whether you are a picture dealer, a collector or, if you prefer, a buyer of pictures, the knowledge required is the same. As a picture dealer, I feel I can best write about picture collecting because a picture dealer is simply a professional collector. The amateur collector may have less knowledge for that reason, but he has the enormous advantage of being able to keep his pictures rather than sell them. Without delving into pre-war history, the last decade alone has witnessed a steady and often rapid increase in the value of pictures which has greatly favoured the wise buyer rather than the seller. In general terms, I see nothing to alter this situation in the foreseeable future, because it is based on an ever greater number of people chasing an ever decreasing supply of pictures. I am referring to pictures of the eighteenth and nineteenth centuries, and I should warn readers that this book does not touch on contemporary paintings of any kind.

Having mentioned rising values in the picture market, the question of investment inevitably follows. Contrary to what you may have been led to believe, the large majority of picture collectors buy from interest in the picture and for something which appeals to them in it. At the same time, they want to know how they stand financially in the unfortunate event of having to part with it – and, with wise purchasing, they can rest assured on this count. The attitude to the painting is that it is firstly a fine painting and secondly, an asset, which will hopefully be passed on to the heirs. I am making this point because the newspapers, with limited space available, tend to concentrate on the price of a picture and the artist's name – not a late Monet, not a large Monet, not a fine Monet, but a £72,000 Monet! The enormously increased newspaper coverage and publicity of all kinds is one of the most obvious symptoms of greater public interest. Investment is an important aspect of collecting and I will discuss it in due course, but this should not ideally be the sole reason for buying pictures. It would be a mistake to forget that the real motives for buying pictures still apply, just as they did when people bought paintings with no idea of gaining from their ownership – at least not in monetary terms.

The choice of what school and what period to collect depends on personal tastes, but certain principles underly all picture buying and it is upon these that I have concentrated. At the same time, I am convinced that it is better to look at an illustration rather than read a description. I have made as large a selection of illustrations as possible, with emphasis on the English school. Our native school has suffered from neglect throughout history, with English eyes so often turned to the Continent. It still offers opportunities and advantages to the new collector, and generally the choice is much wider. In calling the chapter discussing these illustrations 'What to Buy' I am merely suggesting possible fields of interest. For ease of obtaining good reproductions, I have mainly selected examples from the records of my firm, to represent the general availability of paintings and drawings. Nearly all of the paintings are reproduced for the first time, which has the advantage of avoiding the familiar examples in museums which are so often illustrated, and where, in any case, the original is easily accessible. I have also tried to give the reader an approximate guide to the prices of the work of the artists, based on 'retail' rather than saleroom values. The examples range from good watercolours under £100 to paintings up to £4,000 or £5,000. In order to make this chapter as up to the minute as possible, I have taken examples only from pictures sold in the last few years, and included some paintings and drawings offered for sale at the time of writing. Nonetheless, it would clearly be impossible for me to anticipate or give guidance on any changes in value which have taken place either since a particular picture was on the market, or changes between now and the time of publication. My hope is that, among the artists of different periods and nationalities, the reader may find a field of interest, or become familiar for the first time with an artist whose work he would like to collect.

Picture collecting is very practical. With obvious exceptions, pictures are neither large nor heavy, but easy to handle and move. Unlike furniture, for example, they take up no floor space. (In fairness to good furniture, I must add that it is the perfect complement to good pictures.) Pictures hang out of reach of small children, and by the time they are old enough to reach them they will understand what they are, and treat them accordingly. Only the minimum of care is needed for pictures to remain in a perfect state of preservation. Apart from their intrinsic qualities, pictures have a wonderful effect on a room. They give atmosphere and decoration in the way that nothing else can, yet they do not overpower. By decoration, I do not mean pictures whose value is purely decorative – these are appropriately called 'furnishing' pictures. Pictures hanging in the home are unlikely to be stolen because they are not easily disguised and sold like jewellery and silver, and would be outside the understanding of most thieves. In any case, they are not

1 Detail from 'A View of Amsterdam' by ABRAHAM STORCK (1635–1710), showing characteristic seventeenth-century *craquelure*.

2 Detail from a painting by JULIUS CAESAR IBBETSON (1759–1817), showing characteristic eighteenth-century *craquelure* and use of impasto.

expensive to insure when you consider that their rise in value each year is probably greater than the annual premium. As assets, they have proved themselves very sound and easily negotiable if the need arises. Their value in enriching the lives of those who live with them is immeasurable.

Even the most modest collector can feel he is following in a long tradition. England has the richest history of private collecting, and no one besides the artist himself is more important than the private collector. The great public galleries have largely been created by the generosity of private collectors, just as artists have relied on them for patronage. Economic circumstances and the pressure of museum purchasing may have restricted the scope of the great collectors, but corporate buying has a long way to go before it would ever equal the achievements of private individuals.

As I have said, whether you become what may be called a 'good collector', will ultimately depend on yourself. Perhaps for this reason, if you do succeed the greater will be your achievement, and you will have found a lifelong pastime, surely the most absorbing, stimulating and satisfying of all.

I Of Blisters, Buttons, Keys and Scumble: Pictures as Physical Objects

Supports

The familiar concept of a picture expert is of someone who at a cursory glance from several feet can tell what a picture is and who painted it. As an idea, it gains credibility through television programmes where experts identify a fifteenth-century Flemish altarpiece from a photograph of a detail of an angel's hand in the background.

One of the most frequent complaints of the baffled beginner is that a knowledge of paintings seems to depend on purely visual recognition of many intangible subtleties of style and form. For example, they argue that with old silver you can easily tell if it is solid, and that there are hall-marks which are readily looked up to tell you its date, origin, and so forth. In the same way, its pitfalls can be found by simple, physical examination. For instance, by feeling the thickness of the sides of a silver teapot with a finger on the inside and thumb on the outside, a beginner would find the thin patch resulting from an original coat of arms having been removed by abrasion – and so a flaw is revealed. Make no mistake, paintings are objects in the same way and a knowledge of their physical make-up is as essential to the real expert as visual and academic training. I have therefore given this aspect of 'knowing' pictures precedence, so that the next chapter may be read in the right vein. I can only give pointers to what is an extensive subject, but I hope they will whet your appetite to find further information for yourself.

There is always the temptation, in treating with even mildly technical matters, to put them in a 'useful' glossary at the end. I have not done so because of the importance of the subject, and also the nagging feeling that no one reads glossaries. Remember that the advantages of gaining all-round knowledge are twofold. In a situation where the old adage *caveat emptor* (buyer beware) still applies as firmly as ever, knowledge protects you from buying bad pictures. At the same time, it immeasurably helps you to understand and appreciate the good pictures you do buy. The days of the ill-informed collector are over.

In this chapter, I want to carry out an imaginary examination of paintings to see what they may consist of in physical terms, and how this may help in identifying and assessing them. The appearance of a painting is often affected by what has been done in the past to conserve or restore it. With this in mind, I have also tried to include some description of the damage which may be caused to paintings and their natural defects arising from age, and how these are overcome by the restorer. In avoiding too much detail, I have made generalizations to which, inevitably, there are exceptions.

When you are confronted with a painting, whether it is supposed to be by such and such an artist or whether it is unknown, examine it closely because its physical properties will yield many vital clues. The first question is what is the picture painted on? All kinds of materials are used for this purpose, copper, linen, paper, and so on, and these are called the 'support'. As you know, the most common is canvas, followed by panel, so I will deal with these in that order. Canvas, which is unbleached linen, forms an ideal base for painting because it is strong, light, and inexpensive, but mainly because it has a suitable surface texture. It can be woven in many different ways and the differences may be very instructive. Leaving for a moment the back of the picture, or rather the back of the canvas, the texture of the canvas can best be seen from the front in a raking light so that the 'grain' can be seen through the paint surface. You will probably notice straightaway that the lines of the weft and weave in an old canvas no longer run in straight lines but tend, towards the edges, to go in fairly even waves. These waves are produced by the slight shrinkage of the canvas, pulling against the nails which hold its edges to the stretcher.[1] These waves have their crests in line with the nails at the edge and their troughs in between. The effects may be irregular depending on the uneven stresses which were woven into the canvas and then aggravated by the way it has been nailed and stretched on to the stretcher. Pronounced waviness and unevenness of this kind are indications of an old canvas, eighteenth-century or earlier.

The type of canvas will mainly depend on how the artist painted and what effects he wanted to produce. For example, an artist seeking a high degree of 'finish' in his painting would, in general, choose a tightly woven, finely grained canvas with a smooth surface. Another artist, painting broadly with free brush strokes, would favour a heavier canvas with tightly woven but strongly textured surface. One of the commonest canvases of this kind is the stout twill canvas used by English portrait painters in the late eighteenth century. The twill or grain often runs diagonally and was ideally suited to the powerful strokes of their big hog brushes – such a canvas is said to have a good 'tooth'. When the occasion presents itself, look at the contrast between a typical French eighteenth-century portrait and an

[1] See below.

English one in terms of the differences in the two canvases, and notice their appropriateness to the two styles of painting.

Looking at another picture, you find that its canvas is completely different from either of these. It is coarsely woven, with an open effect, from threads of much greater thickness, and there are lumpy unevennesses every so often. The surface is much more obviously criss-crossed or square woven, and altogether the resultant surface texture has unmistakable characteristics. On such a canvas, a typical seventeenth or eighteenth-century Italian or Spanish picture would be painted. Again, the way the picture is painted, the way the brush has been used, is related to the type of canvas available in those countries at that date. Canvases give clues to nationality as well as to date.

I hope you will not feel, thus far, plunged into technicalities because these differences in old canvases are really no more complicated than choosing between a tweed and a worsted for a new suit.

Canvases are usually nailed round a stretcher, a simple wooden framework whose sides and cross pieces are slotted together to allow them to be expanded and so tauten or stretch the canvas, as the name implies. Stretchers are expanded by the small wooden wedges, called keys, found at each slotted join, being tapped firmly into place with a small hammer. Canvases contract and expand and generally move about, so that if they are stretched too tight, or 'over-keyed', the friction between the back edge of the canvas and the stretcher will in time break the canvas. Conversely, a painting where the canvas has become too slack can deteriorate, apart from being distracting to anyone looking at it. If you turn a painting around and find that the stretcher seems old and has no slotted joins and therefore no keys, but is simply a rectangle of four pieces of wood nailed together, it may well be the original eighteenth or early nineteenth-century stretcher. One way of telling the age of a canvas would be to look at the nails fastening the stretcher together, and those round the edges holding the canvas. If they are handmade nails, with heads of irregular shape and size, the stretcher is very probably eighteenth or early nineteenth century. If you feel I am carrying things a bit far when it comes to taking nails into account, I can only reply that an expert would never neglect to do so. I have read how, before the war, a very well prepared and painted forgery of a Frans Hals was easily detected by X-ray. The forger had thought to add authenticity to his old panel by putting battens on the back, which he nailed through from the front of the panel. Although the nail heads were covered by the priming and paint, the X-ray showed them to be modern machine-made ones of the present century. (See A. P. Laurie, *The Technique of the Great Painters*, 1949.) An old English stretcher would generally be made of pine, whereas a Continental stretcher is usually made of a fruit wood, but there are no hard and fast rules. Even if the stretcher is not the original one, always look carefully at stretchers because they may bear identifiable makers' marks, or have on them interesting labels, inscriptions, collectors' marks,[1] and other valuable clues such as customs stamps. One of the most familiar marks on the back of stretchers and panels are the black stencilled letters and numbers of Christie's. Every picture sold at Christie's is given a code number, usually consisting of two or three letters and two or three numerals. Their records can yield interesting information about the date and outcome of a picture's sale at Christie's. In fairness to the staff, enquiries for research of this kind should be as limited as possible.

[1] You may be able to identify a collector's mark by consulting Frits Lugt, *Les Marques de Collections*, 1921.

A sensible thing is to leave your query with a member of the staff for him or her to look up the number when there is a convenient time, and pass on the answer to you. Having mentioned stretcher marks, I must clarify one point. These makers' stamps and other markers have nothing to do with what is generally understood by stretcher marks, which are lines on the front of the canvas resulting from the canvas sagging against the stretcher in the way already described. These lines are easily seen and tend to become very pronounced if the canvas stays against the stretcher continually.[1]

Re-lining

If you have turned the painting round to look at the stretcher, why not look at the canvas from the back at the same time, instead of from the front as I have been describing? Surely it would be easier. Here the answer is quite simple, because the back of the original canvas has usually been hidden by the lining canvas.

Canvases are lined for a variety of reasons, and this process can affect the picture's appearance. Hence, it is as well to understand what lining means. When a painting is lined, the original canvas is stuck down on to a second or lining canvas and the two are bonded together either with a paste or composition, or with wax. If the painting has already been lined at some time in its history, this old lining canvas has to be taken off and the remains of the adhesive which held it, before the original can be put on a new lining canvas; second and subsequent linings are called re-linings. The most obvious reason for lining is when an umbrella, catapult or what have you has put a hole in a picture. Very often, this damage can be repaired to good effect and, according to where it occurs in the picture, may or may not

[1] The inside front edges of stretchers should be bevelled to avoid the canvas sagging against a sharp edge.

constitute a serious flaw. A painting does not have to be punctured to need re-lining. The original canvas may have become fragile, uneven, or be failing to support the picture properly. Alternatively, the stretcher marks may have become too pronounced, or a holly berry from bygone Christmas decorations which has fallen down behind the picture can lodge between canvas and stretcher and, in time, cause a large bump which can only be corrected by lining. Stretcher keys drop out from the top corners and lodge themselves in the same way.

The lining or re-lining of a canvas need have no effect on the picture itself and does not necessarily mean there is anything whatsoever wrong with it. However, bad lining can be very harmful, because like any other skilled job, it can be done the right and wrong way. The traditional method is to take the original canvas, which has been cut off its stretcher, and put a protective layer of paper on the surface. The picture is then ironed from the front on to the lining canvas which has been first stretched and prepared with the adhesive. Ironing sounds alarming, but heat is essential if the two canvases are to be firmly bonded together and air bubbles prevented from forming between them. The degree of heat and the amount of pressure will be carefully controlled according to the type of painting. When a picture has a strong texture in the paint, the re-liner will often use a cloth or other padding between the iron and the surface so as to apply the necessary pressure without flattening out the surface effects which the artist intended. An area of paint which is thickly put on, and stands up from the surface, is called 'impasto' (as we shall see when discussing techniques). Nineteenth-century re-liners and more recent unskilled hands have often flattened and crushed this impasto in the course of lining, and this obviously detracts from the appearance of the picture. A well-lined painting should be firmly bonded to the lining canvas, but at the same time, retain the original surface texture of the paint.

An alternative method of lining is by means of a vacuum table. Here, the adhesive is wax-based, and the two canvases are joined by placing them in an airtight container from which the air is pumped out by an electric pump. The resultant vacuum causes the canvases to stick firmly together. A disadvantage of this method is that, should the picture need re-lining at some future date, it may be very difficult to remove the old wax-bonded lining canvas.

Whichever method is used, the job is completed by cutting the lining canvas to leave a margin all round for nailing back on to the picture stretcher or to a new one if necessary. The back of a new lining canvas is often stained down so that it may not be obvious if the picture has been lined or not. However, if you look at the picture out of its frame, you will clearly see the edge of the original canvas and the margin of newer canvas with its new nails holding it to the stretcher.

Picture lining is a fascinating craft of which I have given you only an outline. I will refer to it again now that it has been explained. Good or bad lining can be to the good or the detriment of a picture's appearance and its state of preservation, two factors with which a buyer must be concerned. Lining is very often the first step in the restoration of a painting, and good lining can rectify what, to the uninitiated, appears irreparable damage. (If you are thinking of buying a painting which you feel requires re-lining and restoration, you must allow for the costs of this work when deciding the purchase price. Yet an understanding of what can be done may enable you to acquire a real bargain because others, less knowledgeable, are frightened off by the superficial condition of a picture.)

Panels

Discussing lining has been a digression, though an essential one, from describing the two main supports of a painting – canvas or panel. As I have said, most pictures have canvas as their support. If you see a painting catalogued in a sale, and there is no mention of medium or support, this is because at the front of the catalogue it will say that unless otherwise stated, pictures are oil on canvas. Of the pictures not painted on canvas, the great majority have wood panels as their support. However, the word 'wood' is seldom used in describing this support, which is referred to generally as panel, or by the name of the wood, oil on oak, and so on. Panel is among the oldest supports for paintings, long before canvas came into use. If you are seeking clues as to a picture's identity, panels are just as rewarding as canvases, if not more so.

Both the type of wood and its thickness can be clues, but again there are exceptions. A typical Italian painting of the fourteenth or fifteenth century, would be painted on an indigenous wood like poplar or a fruitwood like lime, and the panel would be an inch or more thick. A typical Flemish picture of the same period would be painted on an oak panel, which would also have a substantial thickness. Although canvas had come into general use by the seventeenth century, oak panels remained predominant in the Flemish and Dutch schools. Even for larger pictures, painters of these schools often used oak panels, and made the necessary joins to overcome the limited width of a single piece. Such joins are a natural part of the make-up of these pictures, and should be accepted as such. The problems joins may cause from the preservation point of view will be discussed presently, together with their remedies. If you examine a Dutch or Flemish seventeenth-century oak panel, you will find it is very thin, about a quarter of an inch thick, in contrast to earlier or, significantly, later ones. The back may have along its length the marks, flat shallow troughs, left by the adze, the tool which was used to thin the panel. Such a panel would almost certainly have bevelled edges all round, again cut by hand, so that there may be slight unevennesses in the width and the slope of the bevel. Out of their frames, not surprisingly, these panels are very fragile because of their thinness and especially if they have a join. Thus, a seventeenth-century Dutch painting should be, with few exceptions, painted on oak; the panel should be slight in thickness and the back edges should be bevelled. If, for example, it is bevelled on the bottom and two sides, but not on the top, it may be that the panel has had a piece broken or cut off at some time. With eighteenth or nineteenth-century pictures the panels may be thicker and, most important, other woods (especially mahogany) were used and the bevelling was sometimes not done.

The best way to appreciate the appearance of a seventeenth-century Dutch oak panel, hand prepared in every way, is to contrast it with a machine-made nineteenth-century mahogany panel. Even without the difference in woods, the precise lines and finish of the later panel would stand out beside the handwrought seventeenth-century one. Of course this is an extreme contrast, but even the differences in cutting and bevelling between a seventeenth-century Dutch panel and an eighteenth-century English one are distinctive apart from any differences in the wood. Such differences may seem trivial technicalities, but you have to bear in mind that two hundred years after the deaths of many of the famous seventeenth-century Dutch masters, painters were still doing pictures in their manner. The pastoral scenes, bathed in golden light, of Aelbert Cuyp

(1620-91)[1] and the strange moonlight effects of Aert Van Der Neer (1603-77), to mention two famous Dutchmen, were both favourite themes for later painters. The unfortunate people who have bought these later productions in the belief that they were acquiring an original could have saved themselves a lot of unhappiness by looking carefully at the back of the panel as well as the front.

Like the backs of old canvases and stretchers, panels may have guild marks, collectors' seals, ink inscriptions and so on. Never hesitate to examine a canvas or panel carefully for any such details, even though you may arouse comment by doing so, and accusations of one-upmanship. I remember once at a saleroom viewing noticing two intense but conscientious gentlemen from the Continent trying to decipher a large red seal which they clearly thought was a famous collector's coat-of-arms and motto, on the back of an early panel. As the picture and its seal were obviously of very dubious authenticity, this ponderous scrutiny of the seal seemed superfluous. A well-known saleroom wag happened to pass by and chided them with the remark, 'Well, what does the seal say, then? Received with thanks?'

Panels have a harder, smoother surface than a canvas, and painters use these properties in a variety of ways, just as we saw them do with different canvases. With priming, which will be discussed shortly, a panel can be made into the smoothest possible surface on which a painting of the highest degree of finish can be painted. Such pictures are built up slowly over many days with minute workings, culminating in a finished picture where no brush stroke is to be seen. Sometimes the painters who work in this manner, who were aptly called in seventeenth-century Holland 'the

[1] One of the best-known and most popular Dutch artists in eighteenth-century England. Many of his finest pictures remain in this country, of which my favourite is the 'View of Dordrecht' in the Iveagh Bequest, Kenwood.

masters of the tight brush', can attain the same results on carefully prepared canvas, but in general their finest achievements have panel as their support. In either case, the support is usually hidden by layers of preparatory priming.

You would probably not find it easy, in the case of highly-finished pictures, to tell at first glance whether they are on canvas or panel, because the support is 'hidden' by both the priming and the built-up or worked-up paint surface. You would certainly not have the same difficulty with pictures by artists who worked on panels in a completely different way. I will take the well-known Dutch landscape painter, Jan Van Goyen (1596-1656) as an example of what might be called, in contrast, masters of the 'loose' brush. In his mature work, Van Goyen used virtually unprimed oak panels, that is, panels with the minimum preparation to receive the paint.[1] Over the smoothed surface of the pale oak, Van Goyen's brush moved freely and rapidly, with a kind of brushwork more akin to drawing in paint or sketching, than to oil painting in the more conventional sense. With this technique, the painter allows the light colour of the panel to show by itself and through thin layers of paint, using it in the way that other artists might employ a colour proper. When you look at a Van Goyen of this kind, two things have happened in the course of time, which will be confusing and make it difficult at first to recognize. Firstly, the oak has darkened considerably and appears a pinkish-brown colour, and secondly, the graining has come through and often appears as tiny dark lines all over the picture, but it is particularly noticeable in the lighter tones of the sky. Many Dutch and Flemish artists of the seventeenth century painted in this fluent,

[1] However, the wood was very well seasoned, joined if necessary with the greatest care, as witnessed by the survival of many seventeenth-century Dutch pictures in a perfect state of preservation.

calligraphic way and deliberately allowed the panel to play a part in the painting of the picture. It is a mistake, still made by some present-day restorers, to touch out these areas where the wood is very noticeable, because they are essentially part of the picture as the artist painted it. To understand the appearance of this type of painting on panel, you must therefore appreciate how it arises.

As supports, panels suffer from their own drawbacks, as opposed to those of canvas, which must be met with appropriate remedies. The principal enemies of pictures on panel are excessive heat or dryness and sudden changes of temperature and humidity, which cause warping. If a panel becomes badly affected by warping (or mishandling for that matter) it will probably crack. As I have said, in fairness to the condition of a picture you must distinguish between such a crack or split and an 'original' join of two or more widths of panel. In large pictures, joins are made in canvases, but these are generally less noticeable than those on panels. Of course, the join itself may be vulnerable when a panel starts to warp. The most common malady caused by warping is when the priming and the paint with it have become detached from the panel and lift up in a bump, called a blister. Blisters are easily seen in a raking light on the surface of a panel, and they can be remedied. If they are left unattended, they will usually increase in size and eventually the paint surface cracks and flakes away. Flaking must always be taken very seriously as it can lead to a rapid deterioration in a picture's condition.

When you look at the back of a panel, you can see what has been done to prevent the movement of a panel or remedy its effects. Sometimes a crack or split is best repaired by opening and re-glueing alone, but more often glueing the edges is accompanied by bonding small blocks of wood across the crack to hold it – these pieces are called 'buttons'.

Alternatively, a butterfly-shaped piece of wood, called a dowel, will be let into each side of the crack, and there are variations of both methods. Sometimes battens of wood run along the whole width of the panel over a join or crack.

A much more elaborate means of holding a panel against warping is to 'cradle' it, with a latticework of slats. This is done by glueing strips of wood evenly along the panel with the grain of the wood. Each piece has slots which are carefully lined up so that cross-pieces can be slid through them, across the grain. Although cradling is much more costly than putting on buttons or dowels, its great advantage is that the cross-pieces which hold the panel are not fixed and permit the panel a limited movement. A panel which is warping has to be coaxed back to the position, and allowed to settle down, never forced. The enemies of panels are often over-efficient central heating or fires. If you have paintings on panel in your collection, take care that they are not warped by being too near radiators, nor suffer from rapid changes of temperature when the heating in a room is suddenly shut off in cold weather, and the contraction of the panel is too rapid as a result.

Panels can, of course, be attacked by worms which leave their tell-tale holes in the back, and if unchecked, will eventually disrupt the paint surface. Contrary to what many people say, if you tap the panel and powder falls out, this is not a certain sign that the panel has worm. The powder may be left by worms which are long since dead. In any case, worm can be treated to kill them, and if necessary, the holes filled with wax to reinforce any weakness caused. If you suspect a picture on panel, or its frame, to be suffering from active worm, do not neglect to ask a restorers' advice lest the picture suffer, and in the meanwhile the worms transfer themselves to the fine piece of antique furniture below.

When a panel or canvas has rotted beyond repair, even

3 WILLIAM ANDERSON (1757–1837)
'The Thames at Rotherhithe'
Watercolour, signed and dated 1790.
Size: 8¼ × 10½ inches

4 JOHN CLEVELEY JNR (1747–86)
'Torre de San Vicente de Belem, on the River Tagus, Lisbon.
Watercolour, signed and dated 1778
Size: 18 × 24 inches
Described and illustrated in colour in *Sea Painters of Britain* by F. G. Roe, plate 4 (F. Lewis, 1947)

5 NICHOLAS POCOCK (1741–1821)
'Launching a fishing boat'
Watercolour, oval, signed and dated 1789
Size: $10\frac{1}{2} \times 14\frac{1}{2}$ inches

6 HENRY MOSES (*c.* 1779–1860)
'Men-o'-War off Eddystone'
Watercolour, oval, signed and dated 14 January 1797
Size: $6\frac{3}{4} \times 8\frac{1}{2}$ *inches*
Lit: A Dictionary of British Marine Painters, by Arnold Wilson

7 HENRY MOSES
'Marine view'
Watercolour, oval, signed and dated 10 January 1797
Size: $6\frac{3}{4} \times 8\frac{1}{2}$ *inches*
Lit: A Dictionary of British Marine Painters, by Arnold Wilson

8 JOHN THOMAS SERRES (1759–1825)
'A view of Leghorn'
Oil on canvas, signed and dated 1799, and inscribed 'Livorno'
Size: $15\frac{1}{4} \times 24$ *inches*

9 THOMAS LUNY (1758–1837)
'Shipping in Southampton Water'
Oil on canvas, signed and dated 1788
Size: $21\frac{3}{4} \times 33\frac{3}{4}$ *inches*

in the case of a canvas beyond relining, the painting can actually be transferred to a new support. Transferring, the most delicate process of picture conservation, is carried out by first protecting and strengthening the paint surface, and then, with the picture face down, the support is taken away, so that the picture can be 'adhered' to a new support. When the canvas has been soaked and lifted, or the panel planed down, the back of the ground or priming is exposed. Transferring may have been necessary because this layer of preparation is persistently coming away from its support, not because the support itself has deteriorated. Because of the hazards and costs involved, transferring is not a common occurrence, but it can be and often is a hundred per cent effective, and preserves a picture whose existence seemed in the balance. For the layman at a restorer's studio during the transfer of a painting, to see the back of the priming of a picture with the impressions of the removed canvas imprinted in it, is a fascinating sight.

I hope you have not found transferring a difficult process to follow, but because it is comparatively rarely used, you will seldom encounter a transferred picture. Transferring draws attention again to the way a painting's structure is made up of layers from the bottom or base to the surface of the picture's varnish. With this fact always in mind, you will understand that transferring, however tricky in practice, is simple in theory, because it involves the separation of the layers of a painting and the replacement of the bottom one.

You have started examining pictures in the way that a painter started preparing them – with the choice of support. Painters who worked almost directly on to the support, like Van Goyen, are exceptions to the general practice, as you will see by comparing their pictures to those of the majority. In fact, Van Goyen and others like him use the colour of the wood as others do the colour of their priming. Normally, when a canvas was stretched or a panel cut and smoothed, it was prepared for painting by applying the priming, to which of course, I have already made several references. Without such preparation, a canvas or panel would generally be too rough in texture and too absorbent for painting on. Even the oak panels of the seventeenth-century Dutchmen were sized to seal the surface against absorbency. The painter, or rather his assistant, would therefore apply one or more of a variety of substances to fill up the graining of the canvas or panel until a surface of the right texture and absorbency had been achieved. Earlier Italian and Northern panel paintings were primed with gesso, which is plaster of paris with size as a binder. The first applications are called the ground and may be quite coarse, but the final layer of preparation on which the paint is to go is called the priming. Primings are generally finely ground white powders in binding liquids, in many cases a white chalk bound with oil or white lead providing a good non-absorbent surface, but their surface when dried may be rubbed down to provide the maximum desirable smoothness. There is a wide variety in the preparation of supports, and the layers of increasingly fine gesso in an Italian primitive's panel, where there is a true ground and priming, may be contrasted to a seventeenth or eighteenth-century picture where only one thin layer has been put on. The terms ground and priming tend therefore to become merged and are often referred to simply as the priming. Pigment can be added to the white priming to produce a final priming whose colouring may determine the overall appearance of the finished picture's colour. Preparing a canvas or panel *in extenso* can be likened to a builder finishing a brick wall, first with coarse rendering and then with a fine finishing plaster. The workmen who prepared the walls of Italian churches and palaces finished with a fine layer of plaster on to and into which the artists painted, a technique called *fresco*, in which the great mural masterpieces of the Renaissance were painted. The choice of priming, its colouring and texture, are so closely linked to the actual painting of a picture, that they may be best discussed in that context.

Technique

Today, the search for originality of means as well as subject matter has produced techniques where the paint is thrown on to the canvas, squeezed on, sprayed on and so forth, so that the term 'technique' in respect of how a picture is painted would seem to have little meaning. Even if developments of this century are excluded, the description of traditional techniques of oil painting with a brush would have to encompass everyone from Van Eyck to Monet.

Yet the beginner must not be deterred, because many basic methods are common to the majority of painters and easily recognized. From recognition of the general the beginner can soon identify the particular, in other words the individual touch of a particular painter. Here is the crux of the problem. The old adage that a painter's technique is as individual and distinctive as a person's handwriting is very true. Often the final attribution of a painting will rest not on the subject matter, nor the colouring, but the character of the individual strokes of the brush, or the handling as it is called. This is what is meant in fictional stories about the art world where the bearded expert declares in a melodramatic voice, 'I see the *hand* of the master in every passage of the canvas.' On a more mundane level, if you query the absence of a signature on a picture where there is reason to expect one, the reply will often be, 'Ah! but surely it's signed all over!'

I remember once a painting was brought to our gallery which was supposed to be by John Constable, but there was no provenance, nor background, to the picture. At first sight, it looked like a late copy after a well-known French eighteenth-century painting in the Wallace Collection by Greuze. Yet the brushwork and the technique as a whole were undeniably like Constable. With paintings of such importance and value, they need ideally to be established by something more than opinions. In this case, there was enough incentive to begin research at the Victoria and Albert Museum, where typescripts of Constable's unpublished correspondence were kept.[1] Eventually, for he was a prodigious letter writer, I found the correspondence which proved the authenticity of the painting. A lady had seen the Greuze at an exhibition and found it reminded her of a lost child. She asked Constable to make a copy for her and send it to her in the Isle of Wight. Constable agreed to do this without charge, and at the same time wrote to a close friend complaining how time-consuming these sort of little favours were! Literary evidence confirmed what the technique of the painting had strongly suggested.

Recognition is a reassuring step on the road to complete familiarity with an artist's work. Fortunately for the beginner, the preparation and painting of pictures has been given some uniformity by the conditions under which artists worked until the nineteenth century. The system of a sound apprenticeship leading to acceptance by a guild or academy meant not only a preservation of a high standard of workmanship but a handing-on of traditional methods. Clearly, no system could ensure the artistic merit of the paintings produced and there were drawbacks, particularly in portraiture, in the monotony of a conventional technical

[1] This fascinating source of information about the author's personal life and work has since been published in six volumes.

approach. A major drawback for beginner and expert alike, in the accepted working methods of the masters, was the frequent use of pupil assistants. They were either 'specialists' like drapery painters, or painters capable of executing a complete picture after the master's design. I will refer to this practice again. It follows that many of the great artists, the innovators around whom the history of art evolves, surprise us by how they paint as much as by what they paint. Much of the beauty of a picture can derive from the way the paint as material is actually handled, so that the surface of a fine picture is pleasing to study at close range. One of my favourite paintings is Rembrandt's famous picture in the Louvre of an ox's carcase. Close to this canvas you see that the surface is richly painted with thick textures and flourishes of the brush, and it is only with difficulty that you restrain yourself from feeling the paint surface with your fingers. Books on Rembrandt will tell you that he has transformed this unusual subject matter into a great painting. What is not emphasized is how, in doing so, he did not rely on a pleasing composition, or a range of beautiful colours, or delightful detail, but on pure painting alone. Rembrandt had many pupils who followed his subject matter, his dramatic lighting, his choice of colour, but with very few exceptions the unique quality of his paint eluded them. Of course, the pursuit and attainment of technical virtuosity may present its own pitfalls. Technique as an end in itself is boring and vacuous, but in general the greater an artist's power of expression, the more forcibly his ideas and invention are put over.

If asked to describe a painting, most of us would begin with the subject matter. Next would be in what medium it is painted. To avoid any confusion as to the different kinds of painting, one should think of paint as a 'dry' raw material in the first place. Paints are synthetically made today, but originally were obtained from the earth in ores and minerals, and from plants, fish, and animals. The pigments were ground to a fine powder (one of the apprentices' tasks) and then needed a 'liquid' to dissolve it, vary its consistency, and so allow the artist to start work. This liquid 'carries' the paint and is often called the 'vehicle' for that reason. The vehicle gives the medium its name. White of egg for tempera painting and water for watercolour[1] were the most common vehicles until the introduction of oil in the fifteenth century. Oil (linseed oil) allowed far greater possibilities to the artist's technique and has always remained the most common form of painting, and the one on which I shall concentrate in this chapter. Need I emphasize again that this part of the chapter is a most summary introduction to the materials and technique of painting? The book mentioned at the end should be consulted for comprehensive information.

A finished 'old master' oil painting of a conventional kind was built up with different layers of paint, or perhaps a better description would be, with different workings. By this means, colours and tones are achieved by the effects of seeing one pigment through a layer of another painted over it. The variety of effect will depend on whether the top layer is clear (transparent) or solid (opaque), how thickly it has been put on and how evenly. Without wanting to confuse things by referring to another medium, I would say that most readers will have used an ordinary watercolour paintbox, with the inside of the lid white-enamelled for mixing colours. A colour in its block or coming thickly out of a tube seems opaque. When you put water with it and make it thin, and then spread it over the lid, the colour changes because it is transparent and the whiteness of the lid shows through it. In the same way, the painter in oils can

[1] This medium is discussed and illustrated in the next chapter.

use the white of the priming to show through passages of his paint. The only difference here is that oil colours divide naturally into opaque and transparent ones, but obviously the transparent colours can be made opaque by mixing. Conversely, while it cannot be made transparent, a colour that is naturally opaque can be thinned out by the amount of oil used. Oil would by itself be too thick for the degree of thinning out needed, so turpentine is used for diluting.

Although you will see many paintings, particularly in the Flemish school, where the artist has used a very light coloured priming, most artists preferred to colour it over to a greater or lesser extent, or actually prime the support with a dark priming. Whatever the colour of a painting's priming, it will usually give a characteristic overall tone or tint to that passage or to the whole picture.

Having decided on the colour of his priming as a base, the artist would usually make some form of preliminary drawing. Either he would make separate sketches and transfer his solutions on to the canvas, or draw his outlines directly on to the priming. Then, in a portrait for example, the figure would be roughed-in in neutral colours, in terms of light and shadow as it were. This is called the underpainting or laying-in. From there, the picture would be worked up either with solid passages of colour, or by the use of opaque colour in a way that allows the colour or priming beneath to show through here and there amid the brush strokes. This sort of brushwork is called scumbling. In the same way, for maximum effect, a dry brush without too much paint, is 'dragged' lightly over the canvas allowing the 'tops' of the canvas to catch the colour and leaving the underneath colour clear in the hollows of the weave. Where transparency is the aim, the painter uses the transparent colours alone over the colour beneath, and appropriately this is called 'glazing'. Glazes are conventionally used in the finishing of a painting just as the highlights are 'worked up to' and put in at the last. A typical finish would therefore involve transparent subtle glazes contrasted with solid, opaque passages and highlights. Often the painter wants to raise the paint up from the surface to suggest depth, variety and texture. Paint raised up in this way is called impasto which, as has already been noted, must be treated carefully when a canvas is re-lined.

Obviously a badly-mixed colour, a glaze which has been allowed to become cloudy, a badly placed stroke of solid paint, are among the many lapses of technique which can mar a picture. Turgid colours and insensitive brushwork belong to poor quality pictures.

Old paintings, if unmolested, are very durable because of the sound preparation and workmanship I have mentioned, but the majority are affected by the passage of time, making them different as we see them today from the day they came from the artists' easels. So when looking at a painting, these natural changes must be taken into account. Such changes can be both a help and a hindrance in identifying and assessing a painting.

Quite simply, the best way to understand pictures in their physical make-up, execution and condition is by looking at them for yourself. I want to give some examples of the terms used in this chapter, by looking at pictures in public collections. For convenience, I have looked at pictures in the National Gallery and the National Portrait Gallery next door. If you live too far from Trafalgar Square to get to these great galleries, no matter. You will find the same sort of painting, in physical terms, in local museums throughout the country.[1] The paintings are not illustrated because photographs cannot show the points under consideration without many detailed close-ups. I have pre-

[1] See next chapter.

ferred to reserve the available illustrations, in the main, for the chapter on what to buy.

Room 6[1] at the top of the National Portrait Gallery provides excellent opportunities for investigating eighteenth-century painters and their techniques. I have chosen this room because the large skylight provides very good daylight.

The principal picture is a full-length portrait of the third Earl of Bute by Sir Joshua Reynolds (1713-92), painted in the 1770s. For the support, Reynolds used a typical English twill canvas (see page 3), with the diagonal weave clearly discernible, which gives the picture a recognizable surface texture. On the left-hand side, below the hat, the waviness of the canvas weave, which I have already discussed, can be seen in the grey stone of the architectural background. In this background, which is naturally less thickly painted than the figure, you can see at close range the lightish colour of the ground or priming beneath the grey of the stonework. The figure is essentially painted in a strong, solid technique, with ample paint built up with powerful strokes, yet close attention to detail in the finishing. Many passages of the costume are very thickly painted with rich impasto, and the effect is one of vitality through the surety of the brush-work. You would decide for yourself that scumbling is used more than glazing in what is basically a 'dry' worked[1] up technique.

Age has affected this picture in two ways. Firstly, like all old paintings, the paint surface is mostly covered by small cracks. Again, you must look closely to see these properly, and a small magnifying glass may be a help. As the oil dried and the paint hardened, it shrank very slightly and produced this cracking, which is called *craquelure*. Broadly

[1] I understand, at the time of writing, that no change in the distribution of pictures in the various rooms is envisaged, but the pictures would, in any case, be easily sought out.

speaking, paintings of different centuries have a distinctive *craquelure* because of their age and the priming which, of course, cracks with the paint. This cracking or *craquelure* is an immense help in recognizing and assessing the authenticity and period of a picture. Figure 1 is a detail from a seventeenth-century Dutch painting,[1] showing characteristic *craquelure* of that century. You can see that it is a fine, even, overall cracking.

Contrast this seventeenth-century cracking with that of the eighteenth century in Figure 2. This detail is taken from a painting[2] of about the same size as the one in the previous illustration. Here the cracking is irregular over the surface, much more widely spaced, and the cracks tend to be larger. The same kind of cracking on a larger scale will be found in the Reynolds portrait. Figure 2 also shows how well the artist has used impasto brushwork to define the clouds and the practised assurance of the handling. In the middle of this sky, there is a point where the cracks run in roughly concentric circles, like a spider's web. This phenomenon is very common indeed and many people ask what causes it. Artists use a maulstick[3] which they hold in the left hand and lean against the painting or the easel. The end of this stick is padded for this purpose. With a maulstick there is a rest on which the artist can steady his right or brush hand. In self-portraits, artists often depict themselves with palette and maulstick in hand, like Rembrandt's famous self-portrait at Kenwood.[4] When an artist rested the maul-

[1] 'A View of the Muntplein, Amsterdam' (detail) from a painting by Abraham Storck (1635-1710).

[2] Detail from a landscape by Julius Caesar Ibbetson (1759-1817), an artist who will be referred to again in Chapter 4.

[3] Or Mahlstick; *Maler* is German for painter.

[4] The Iveagh Bequest, Kenwood, Hampstead. The house and grounds, together with a magnificent collection of paintings, were given to the nation in 1927 by the Earl of Iveagh, better known as Edward Cecil Guinness, justly famous as a brewer.

stick lightly on the canvas, it could make an imperceptible depression in the newly-primed surface, which, in the course of time, results in cracking of this kind.

An understanding of *craquelure* can be especially helpful with one of the commonest pitfalls – the falsely signed painting. If there is cracking where the picture is signed, the lines of the cracks will run through the paint of the signature, because it is contemporary with the rest of the paint surface. If the signature is a later addition, it will go over the cracks of the original paint surface,[1] tending to interrupt and obscure them. In the very few serious modern forgeries of old paintings, the forgers have taken great care to simulate the appropriate *craquelure*. This has been done by working over old paintings and using heat to make the old cracks come through the new paint surface as it is rapidly dried. Alternatively, the forger has stripped off an old painting in order to use an old canvas and then re-primed it and painted his copy. He then has tried to make the new paint and priming crack in a convincing way, either by rolling the canvas up in different directions, or by rolling a smooth, heavy object like a billiard ball over the surface to crack it. This would not appear to have much effect until the paint has dried and contracted to bring out the cracking. Drying out would normally take years, so an oven was used to dry the paint quickly in the hope that it would crack where cracking had been induced artificially. Success, whatever the method, has been very limited indeed. What is more important, is to spot supposedly seventeenth-century paintings with a pronounced eighteenth-century *craquelure*. When, today, you see art students copying pictures in the National Gallery or Victoria and Albert Museum, bear in mind that copying has always been part of a painter's training, just like drawing from the nude

[1] See Chapter 3, on saleroom cataloguing.

figure – even more so in the schools and academies of the past, particularly in the eighteenth and nineteenth centuries, not to mention the untold numbers of amateur artists. Many thousands of these 'exercises' are still around for the unwary.

After looking at only one picture, I have deliberately paused for an explanation and illustration of *craquelure*, because of its importance among the easily noticed technical aids to recognition, and I will refer to it again. The beginner would be wise to develop his knowledge of *craquelures* by making his own comparisons and investigations. When doing so in public galleries, it is as well to reassure the attendant that you are merely looking closely at the picture and that this is not a prelude to touching it.

Returning to Room 6 at the National Portrait Gallery, when you have looked at the Reynolds, turn to Gainsborough's portrait of the first Lord Amherst. Here is a picture of roughly the same date as the Reynolds, but different in appearance, because it is not painted in the same way. The canvas is much finer in texture, and in the very right-hand top corner a small part of the white priming is still visible. Gainsborough covered this priming thinly with a beautiful pale purple-grey as a base colour. This base determines the delicate note of the flesh colour, and is left without further covering in parts of the hair. Every part of the painting is thinly painted in delicate glazes with few opaque passages and only occasional flicks of impasto as in the insignia on the red coat and in the highlights of the hair. It is obvious that Gainsborough used turpentine to dilute his paint for these very thin glazes which achieve such luminosity. The background is particularly thinly painted, with the purple of the base colour showing through rich raw umber[1] (grey-green) and burnt umber

[1] Colours whose names derive from their first use in Italy when they came from the province of Umbria. Raw siena (dark yellow) and burnt siena (reddish brown) are other examples.

(rich brown). Gainsborough's portrait appears very fragile compared to the robust opacity of the Reynolds. Indeed, Gainsborough's technique and predominant use of glazing has more in common with French eighteenth-century painters than with the conventional English technique as represented by Reynolds.

When you have looked at the quality of these leading painters' work in terms of technique and execution, contrast them with the two school copies in the same room. The oval portrait of Wentworth after Reynolds seems lifeless, and the portrait of Lord Lyttelton after Gainsborough lacks his transparency and brushwork.

Another example of Gainsborough in the next room, Room 4, a portrait of the fourth Duke of Bedford, is painted on a different base colour, of a rich, dark red-brown. Again it is not an opaque ground, but one where the whiteness of the priming beneath is all important. In the same way, this base colour sets the tone of the picture. On the right side of the face, it is barely covered with glazes and so a warm red shadow is produced. One characteristic of Gainsborough's style, rather than his technique, is very pronounced in this example. If you look closely at the pupils of the eyes, they are painted square. The effect, when you step back, is to make the eyes appear more natural and animated than if he had painted round in fidelity to nature.

It goes without saying that if you are interested in a particular artist, you must learn to recognize the different stages of his development. The two examples of Gainsborough cited so far are both painted in his later style of fluent, light brushwork. In Room 5, there is a self-portrait by him (of 1759) where you can see indications of the kind of brushwork which becomes so free and loose in the later pictures. This self-portrait is, like the Bedford picture, painted over a red ground or base colour.

I said that age affected these portraits in two principal ways, and I have described the cracking as the first of them. The second concerns the changes in the pigments and oil medium which, like the *craquelure*, is a natural result of ageing, and not in any way a damage which has been inflicted on the picture.

Unbeknown to the artists at the time of their use, certain colours have not lasted well and in some cases have disappeared almost entirely from a picture. Among the most common of these 'fugitive' colours are organic colours which have a carbon content, and many of these were used for glazes. Crimson lake, carmine and madder, are typical examples. The paleness of Reynolds' flesh colour, which can be seen to some extent in the Bute portrait, has been greatly accentuated by the gradual loss of the red carmine pigment. You will be able to find other examples of how the use of fugitive colours has resulted in changes in a picture's present-day appearance.

A basic colour on the artist's palette was white lead, a strong opaque white pigment. Unfortunately, white lead becomes increasingly translucent with age, changing the colour with which it may have been mixed and letting the light of the priming show through to a greater extent. Linseed oil as a vehicle tends to yellow with age and also becomes increasingly translucent.

In the later Gainsborough portraits, the extreme transparency in certain parts, which is more than the artist intended and might suggest that the paint had become thin, is in fact due to the way that the oil and the white, used to render greater opacity, have become more translucent in the course of nearly two centuries. One of the most familiar results of increased translucency is that the underpainting, not of course intended to be seen, has become visible. In this way, you will sometimes see how the artist has changed his mind and his first idea, which he then painted out and altered, shows faintly through. The line of a sitter's head may have been changed, or the placing of a tree in a sky, or the position of an arm, and you may see the 'ghost' of this alteration. These artist's alterations are called *pentimenti* after the Italian word, *pentirsi*, to repent. There are no rules to say in which pictures these changes will occur, nor how many of them. Generally speaking, the results of fugitive colours, the yellowing of oil, the increased translucency of oil and white lead and the resultant exposure of *pentimenti*, although they may sound rather alarming, need not by any means be too disturbing to the appearance of a picture, nor detrimental to its condition.

There is an unhappy exception. In the later eighteenth, and particularly in the first half of the nineteenth century, artists introduced bitumen to their armament of colours. This is a deep brown pigment made from asphaltum, which appeared to offer a superbly rich colour, particularly useful for shadows, brown foliage, and generally for glazing. Unfortunately, bitumen never hardens properly, spreading where it was not intended to be, and cracks very heavily indeed, often producing a shrivelled looking surface. Bitumen has undoubtedly led to the deterioration of many pictures, and the disfigurement of many more. It figures high on the list of restorers' nightmares. Unfortunately, Reynolds in his later period often used bitumen, and thus set an example to his many pupils and followers. Reynolds was an admirer of Rembrandt, although he did not admit to it in his discourses delivered to the Royal Academy, and tried perhaps to emulate the Dutchman's rich browns by using bitumen.

The wide cracks and molten surface of bitumen are unmistakeable, and its presence is obviously helpful in dating a picture. By the same token, if you are offered a mid-eighteenth century painting with cobalt blue featuring among the colours, it would require an explanation because cobalt blue was not invented until 1802.

I have referred to sketching, laying-in, and under-painting, in the preparation of an eighteenth-century painting. If you are uncertain about these first stages of a picture, it would be essential to look at two or three other portraits. In the room full of portraits of members of the Kit Kat Club, painted by Sir Godfrey Kneller (1649-1732) in the 1720s, number 20, of Richard Boyle, is unfinished. The larger part of the grey-green ground is not covered, but the indications of drawing of the wig and shoulders are quite clear, as are the laying-in with lights and darks. This is the clearest example of how this ground colour, which is fairly opaque covering the priming, conditions the appearance of the nearly completed flesh colour. Kneller's procedure was the standard one for much of eighteenth-century portraiture, although artists like Ramsay and Gainsborough were obvious exceptions.

Sir Thomas Lawrence (1769-1830) may be said to mark the transition from eighteenth to nineteenth-century portraiture. As before, I am taking portraiture as representative of painting in general. In Rooms 13 and 14, there are unfinished portraits by Lawrence of George IV and William Wilberforce. In the former, the priming has been lightly coloured over by a pinkish-brown, and in the latter by a light grey, as ground colours, and they are both very light. Nineteenth-century artists favoured a light ground, and a brighter, more sparkling palette, as you may see in these pictures. Lawrence's handling was so assured and rapid – his portrait of Lady Callcott (Room 14) was painted in two hours – that his technique risks being too facile. Again, the reader would best compare and contrast for himself this technique and palette with either Reynolds' or Gainsborough's work.

10 GEORGE SMITH OF CHICHESTER (1714–76)
'The First Premium landscape painting of 1760, with portraits of the three Smith of Chichester brothers'
Oil on canvas
Size: $30\frac{1}{2} \times 38\frac{1}{2}$ inches

11 GEORGE & JOHN SMITH OF CHICHESTER
'Returning from Market'
Oil on canvas,
Signed
Size: 12×17 inches

12 GEORGE SMITH OF CHICHESTER
'Winter Landscape'
Oil on canvas
Signed
Size: $12\frac{1}{2} \times 17$ *inches*

13 THOMAS JONES (*c.* 1730–1803)
'Landscape with figures and a Boat on a Lake'
Oil on canvas
Signed
Size: 19×24 *inches*

14 JOSEPH FARINGTON (1747–1821)
'Basildon Church and Friary from Streatley Hill, Berks'
Watercolour
Signed and dated 1792
Size: $8\frac{1}{2} \times 11\frac{7}{8}$ inches

15 SAMUEL H. GRIMM (1734–94)
'Shire Green and Grenoside, Yorkshire'
Watercolour
Signed and dated 1781
Size: 15×21 inches

16 WILLIAM PAYNE (1760–1815)
'Weymouth and Portland'
Watercolour
Signed
Size: $11\frac{3}{4} \times 16$ *inches*

17 MOSES GRIFFITH (1749–*c.* 1810)
'Llanbedr Hall, Denbighshire, 1805'
Watercolour
Signed and dated 1 August 1805, and inscribed on reverse
Size: $11\frac{1}{2} \times 15\frac{1}{2}$ *inches*

The early nineteenth century saw the introduction of artists' colourmen, supplying ready-prepared colours in tubes, brushes and other materials. This development coupled with the romantic idea of painting as a 'self-expression', left the studio hand or assistant more or less redundant. Thus, nineteenth-century paintings tend to be entirely by the artist, without the participation of drapery hands and other assistants as in seventeenth and eighteenth-century practice.

Within the Portrait Gallery, needless to say, there is considerable scope for looking at different materials and the ways in which artists have used them. If you go next door to the National Gallery, the possibilities are endless. I would like to draw attention to three more paintings in this context. They are, like the portraits, of a kind to be found in many other art galleries in England and abroad.

Rubens' (1577-1640) working methods provide many problems of attribution and assessment for the scholar. Like Reynolds, he was at the head of a large studio of assistant pupils, but on a much bigger scale. Often Rubens himself would make small oil sketches in preparation for an altarpiece or a cycle of historical pictures for palaces and churches. These sketches had a twofold function; they could be shown to the client for his approval and then passed to assistants as a model from which to produce a full-scale painting. Naturally, Rubens' work did not necessarily end with the painting of the sketch, as he might put the finishing touches to the picture itself. The technique of Rubens' finished pictures is easily seen in the Gallery, with much reproduced pictures like 'Le Chapeau de Paille' portrait of his wife. The use of the light ground, the fluency of the brushwork, the strong colour, became characteristics of much of Flemish painting, such was his influence. Yet, the essence of an artist's technical and artistic abilities are sometimes better illustrated by his first and most spontaneous thoughts on a given subject. For this reason, you may learn more from preliminary works, even though they may be very slight and on a small scale.

Room 14 contains a very typical Rubens sketch, done in preparation for one of the paintings of a series commissioned by Charles I in 1635 for the ceiling of the Banqueting Hall at Whitehall. The subject is a Deification or Apotheosis, which is particularly suitable for ceilings involving, as it does, the carrying up to the heavens of the subject, in this instance the Duke of Buckingham. On the surface of the panel, which is almost circular, the join in the wood is just noticeable. Rubens liked to cover the white priming with a tawny, transparent colour, and then work predominantly in browns, greys, and yellows. The word used to describe this muted palette without colour proper, is *grisaille*. In fact, Rubens' sketches are not usually pure *grisailles*, but rather, like this example, finished with touches of colour. Over the smooth surface of the panel with its priming and base colour, Rubens' brush moved with the greatest speed and assurance, using thinned transparent colour, in a way which might accurately be called drawing in paint. Even if you were completely unfamiliar with Rubens and his work, the skill and rapidity of his draughtsmanship, the effortless foreshortening of figures in many different attitudes, and the sense of vitality throughout the execution, would, I think, lead you to feel that here is the work of a great painter. In the bottom right-hand part of this sketch you will see how Rubens decided to change the placing of one of the small *putti* and flicked paint over the figure he had done, leaving it barely visible like a *pentimente* in a finished picture.[1]

It may seem strange to take a rapid oil sketch as an

[1] Notice too, how the cracking of this seventeenth-century picture on panel, thinly primed and thinly painted, differs from the other examples.

example of Rubens' technique, but the extraordinary fact is that his full-scale paintings, though obviously more finished and detailed, are painted in the same way. Both Rubens' manner of painting and his strong palette set the pattern for much of Flemish painting and that of other schools. An amateur collector is unlikely to have more than an academic interest in Rubens, but it is as well to be familiar with the type of execution which Rubens initiated, and which was followed by many lesser painters whose work is accessible. When you go to the Banqueting Hall in Whitehall and see the finished painting *in situ*, you may agree that Rubens' first small sketch on panel is more exciting than the completed canvas. An artist's first steps in the creative process, as seen in drawings and oil sketches, may therefore be more desirable than the greater, but less spontaneous, effort of the finished work. Obviously this applies especially to artists like Rubens, whose finished pictures are not necessarily from their own brush.

An artist of a very different kind who was also head of a workshop was Antonio Canaletto (1697-1768). Most galleries have an example of Canaletto's different views – often called *vedute* from the Italian – of Venice. No other city approaches Venice in its consistent appeal to the imagination of artists and to the countless people who go there or who are intrigued by such paintings, to do so. Apart from the extra appeal and importance which topographical interest may give to any landscape or architectural painting, scenes of Venice are unique because the city, to outward appearances, has changed very little indeed in the course of centuries.

Because of the inseparable connection between Canaletto and his native city, it may seem inappropriate to refer to a painting from his English period, the 'View of Eton College', in Room 13. I do so because, at the time of writing, this famous painting had recently been cleaned, providing the best example of a Venetian eighteenth-century painting. The canvas grain has that distinctive square weave which has already been mentioned. Throughout the sky, you can see between the brush strokes glimpses of the characteristic red-brown priming so favoured by Venetian artists, which, from a distance, gives the appearance of overall warmth. Canaletto paints fatly and solidly in a bold stroke, and even small figures are put in with terrific verve. His highlights are the most distinctive feature of his 'handwriting' as a painter. Instead of being flicks or dashes of brightness they are tiny, neat dots. In a mysterious way, they enliven the unfailing accuracy and detail of his buildings. Particularly with Canaletto, discoloured varnishes sunk into the canvas, as in several Venetian scenes in the same room, can rob the paintings of their rich colouring and the special sparkle which Canaletto's highlights give to his pictures, and which are so often a glaring parody in the hands of his imitators.

The success of Canaletto with English patrons[1] in the eighteenth century had important artistic consequences through his influence on one of the principal English marine and topographical artists, Samuel Scott (*c*.1702-72), passed on to a lesser extent to Scott's pupil, William Marlow (1740-1813).

Before leaving the Venetian room, it is interesting to contrast Canaletto's technique with that of his contemporary, Guardi. Here, coarsely ground pigments may lead to a paint surface which can only be described as gritty. Guardi's smaller *vedute*, and where the scene is an imaginary one, *capricci*, are an interesting blend of glazing with flashes of opaque colour, entirely different from Canaletto, apart from the obvious difference in their actual brushwork. The canvases, primings and surface textures of these major

[1] The Royal Collection at Windsor is the finest and most extensive.

figures are shared by minor Venetian and other North Italian artists in the eighteenth century. These may be of direct, or acquisitive interest to the collector now that the great names have passed so far beyond reach.

To understand the revolution in the way of painting which came about in the nineteenth century, it would not be necessary to cite any particular example. I have already mentioned the end of the pupil-assistant, but this is a change in practice rather than method. Painters gradually dispensed with underpainting and the systematic build-up of glazes and scumbles so typical of the 'old masters' technique. Direct painting, as this is called, became the order of the day, and by and large has remained so. Paintings were started and finished at one working. The complete change in technique was based on a new approach by the artist to his subject matter. Since effects of great spontaneity and immediacy are typical of direct painting at its best, it was ideally suited to the Impressionist attitude of immediate, unpretentious response to everyday subjects informally presented to the observer. For subject matter that was fleeting in itself, a style of painting dependent on suggestion, rather than detailed statement, was appropriate and in harmony with a very direct 'attack'. Details were put into the paint that was still fresh and wet on the canvas, demanding a first-time accuracy of brushstroke because there was no second or subsequent working to alter a false touch. To do so immediately, when painting with pure colours, would mix one colour with another at the edges, producing a tell-tale smear of nondescript colour.

Allied to their new technique was a new approach to colour. Just as the Dutch still-life and flower painters in the seventeeth century developed their art against a scientific background of research into botany and optical instruments, so the Impressionists evolved their ideas at a time when the properties of light were being closely studied. Two basic principles guided their choice and use of colour. They rejected black from their palette, creating the purity of colour and lightness of key which are the hallmarks of Impressionism. In place of the familiar dark shadows, mixed with blacks and browns, of the studio painter, they thought in terms of their outdoor painting. In strong sunlight, they saw that the shadow of an object of whatever colour was tinged with the complementary colour. If you take one of the primary colours, red, yellow or blue, the mixture of the other two is said to be its complementary. Thus purple or violet, the mixture of red and blue, is the complementary of yellow, green of red, and orange of blue. So, the brilliant yellow wheatfields and haystacks of Monet cast their purple shadows. Colours and values vary with the intensity of light, hence the paintings the Impressionists did of the same subject at different times of day. Shadows were also modified by the colour on which they fell and the reflected light from any adjacent colourful things.

They also realized that the fall of light on areas of a solid colour could be made more lively by using strokes of different shades of the colour side by side, or juxtaposed, as it is called. They also made the same use of the juxtaposition of small dabs of two different primary colours – for a green field, dabs of blue and yellow. At close range, these colours appear quite separate, but seen from a distance, they are merged by the eye and produce a brilliant green. Neutral colours could be suggested in the same way by putting a primary and its complementary together – red and green or blue and orange make excellent greys. These ideas of juxtaposition were carried to their extreme form by the Pointillist group headed by Georges Seurat (1859-91).

If the Impressionists sought greater life in colour seen in daylight and reflected light, they also recognized that the shape or outline of an object changes according to the light in which it is actually seen. Things were therefore painted as they appeared and not as they were known to be.

A common mistake when discussing nineteenth-century techniques is to overestimate the inventiveness of the French Impressionists. Their achievements were actually the culmination of a long evolution in which Constable and Turner played a very important part. Nor should the technique of the nineteenth century be too sharply contrasted or separated from what had gone before. You have only to make the familiar comparison between Manet and the seventeenth-century artists, Frans Hals and Velasquez whom he admired, to realize how these so-called old masters anticipated many of the innovations of the nineteenth century. Since the introduction of modern paints, all conventional painters have been confronted with the same palette and brushes, whose apparent limitations lead to new experiments which widen still further the scope of the term 'oil painting'.

I have tried to introduce some aspects of the structure and techniques of painting. Clearly, it is an extensive subject which deserves close attention from the informed collector. One book on this subject, outstanding for its conciseness and clarity, is to be strongly recommended. This is *The Painter's Workshop* by W. G. Constable. If one pursues such knowledge and remembers to look at paintings in the light of it, one will enjoy great advantages over fellow collectors.

2 More Looking and Learning

Museums and Books

This short chapter on the importance to the beginner of museums and books may seem much more palatable than the preceding technical chapter. But that chapter should be carefully read. It may produce resentment at such a detached, clinical, approach to paintings. Where is the reaction of the mind and emotions to creative expression?

In placing such emphasis on the physical aspects of paintings, I do not, for a moment, forget their other properties, nor should you. The structure, materials, and execution of a painting are an integral part of its creation. None the less, there is a tendency in much that is written to ignore them and to imply a separation between thought and feeling on the one hand, and the means by which they are transferred from the artist to his canvas.

For the training of the eye, there can be no substitute for looking at paintings, as often and in as great a variety as possible. Obvious as this may be, insufficient use seems to be made of public art galleries, which represent to the beginner, great untapped storehouses of knowledge. To derive the most benefit and enjoyment from your visits to museums, reading is essential. If, hypothetically, a choice had to be made between looking at paintings in a gallery or reading an art book, I would always choose to see an original rather than read about it. To find our way in the vast history of painting, we rely first and foremost on a visual repertoire, which needs to be constantly augmented and refreshed. I have often heard it asked, in response to this kind of statement, 'What is the point of studying paintings by Rembrandt, Rubens, Gainsborough and many more, when you will never be able to buy or own an example of their work?'

The answer is twofold. In the first place, there is quality. By studying the work of the greater artists, the eye becomes accustomed to appreciate good painting. In a museum the choice is to some extent made for you, because the presence of the paintings in the museum is evidence of their fine quality. One learns from this pre-selection, and so progresses to make personal judgments away from museums amongst a group of pictures with no name tablets, and without a catalogue to help you. Initially, it is better to try to distinguish good from bad, rather than concentrate on recognizing a given artist's work. It follows that the former will help you with the latter. Secondly, the style of an important artist probably had far-reaching effects among the lesser artists of his period. These lesser figures are the ones which may be within your reach for your own collection, and both in their recognition and understanding, you would be at a disadvantage if you were not familiar with the source of their basic inspiration.

It would be unfair to compare every painting by an artist to an example in a great public gallery. The gallery's picture was probably acquired years ago, when a wider choice was available, and the selection was the considered decision of several experts. Yet, if you can conjure up in your mind's eye a mental picture of a painting you know in a gallery, it gives you a firm basis or point of departure in discussing or looking at other examples of a painter's work.

I am thinking not so much of the great public collections where masterpieces tend to predominate, but of collections where lesser artists' work is represented.

For example, the collector of watercolour drawings[1] should look at the national collection of watercolours in the Victoria and Albert Museum. Only a very small proportion of this comprehensive collection is hung in the galleries at any one time. To see drawings not on view, you must visit the department of Prints and Drawings, quite a small room, and fill in the familiar slip with the names of the artists you want to see. You will, of course, need the catalogue of the collection. Arranged alphabetically, and with useful biographical information about each artist, this book is a valuable work of reference in itself. There will not be many occasions when, in your watercolour collecting, you will encounter the work of an artist who is unrepresented in the collection.[2] There is also a complete index of subject matter, portraits, and place names, with small illustrations of some of the more important items. As with many museums, the catalogue was the work of a previous generation, published in 1927, and has yet to be re-published in revised form. The V. & A. (as it is usually called) gains new acquisitions constantly and these are covered by annual supplements to the catalogue.

One of the most important assets of the collection is the unrivalled group of drawings[3] by J. R. Cozens (1752-97), one of the greatest exponents of the medium, whose work was widely influential. Examples from this group are reproduced in any discussion of Cozens and in many surveys of the history of watercolour painting.

[1] See below, Chapter 4.

[2] See Henry Moses, Chapter 4.

[3] Although watercolours are the result of painting with watercolour, they are usually referred to as watercolour drawings, or simply 'drawings'. See Chapter 4.

A word of advice about visiting the V. & A. A proportion of the collection is always out on loan to another gallery or to an exhibition, or withdrawn for cataloguing, photographing or remounting. If, therefore, you have a particular purpose in mind, it is sensible to write or telephone in advance to ensure that what you want to see is available. I speak from bitter experience. Although the museum itself is open on weekdays from 10 a.m. to 6 p.m. and from 2.30 p.m. to 6 p.m. on Sundays, the Prints and Drawings department, with the usual staff shortage problems, has the following open hours: 10 a.m. to 4.50 p.m. on weekdays, with a closure from 1 p.m. to 2 p.m. for lunch, and it is closed on Sundays.

Those interested in watercolours should also try to visit the British Museum Prints and Drawings Department, which has a fine, but less extensive, collection than the V. & A.[1]

Although I am not proposing in this Chapter to duplicate the information of the excellent guides produced by each museum for its own collection, I could not mention the V. & A. without referring to the Constable collection. I do so because the V. & A. is a most unusual museum, a gathering of the contents of several normal-sized museums of diverse kinds. Visitors, especially those from abroad with limited time available, have been known to exhaust themselves in the vastness and diversity of the great rooms, and to come away never having been to the first floor picture galleries. The collection of Constable's work has no parallel, a priceless representation of a fundamental figure in the whole history of landscape painting. Constable's name is loosely attached to thousands of paintings with which he had nothing whatsoever to do. Yet the borderline between

[1] The special feature of the British Museum watercolour collection is, of course, the Turners.

his closest imitators and his genuine work can be deceptive. For example, F. W. Watts (1800-1870)[1] is an artist who can superficially bear a close resemblance to Constable. For the collector, familiarity with Constable's genuine work and the mannerisms of his style of painting would be valuable, not only in the obvious sense as a safeguard against unauthentic work, but for the discovery of unknown paintings and drawings. The same might be said for any artist of course, but it is particularly relevant with Constable whose extensive output included so many small, rapid, sketches in oils, water-colours, pencil and charcoal, and who worked in many different parts of the country. The Constable collection offers another excellent opportunity of contrasting an artist's large-scale 'formal' oil paintings with his sketches.

Today, when Constable's large oil paintings are no longer available, and his small sketches, such as cloud studies are valued in thousands rather than hundreds, you may feel that your only chance of owning an example of his work would be to discover one in the way I have envisaged. Yet his wonderful pencil studies are still accessible to the modest collector.[2]

Unless you knew in advance, there would be no reason for expecting to find a special collection of a Suffolk-born[3] artist's work in the V. & A. Other museums offering an opportunity to see an outstanding collection of an artist's work are more predictably located. Thus, you should never go to Derby without seeing the Museum's group of works by Joseph Wright of Derby (1734-97), although of course his pictures may be seen in the Tate Gallery and elsewhere. By the same token, a collector seriously interested in the

[1] Not to be confused with G. F. Watts (1817-1904) the Victorian historical and allegorical painter and sculptor.

[2] See Chapter 4.

[3] John Constable (1776-1837) was born at East Bergholt, Suffolk.

great Norwich school would be at a disadvantage for never having seen the superb examples in the Norwich Castle Museum, nor would the student of the greatest Welsh-born artist, Richard Wilson (1714-82) be content without visiting the largest existing collection of his work at the National Museum of Wales, Cardiff. The incredible wealth of museums and galleries in the British Isles means that wherever they live, readers will have access to a worthwhile museum. When you travel, both at home and abroad, try to profit from the opportunities of seeing fine paintings. An indispensable publication for all museum-goers is the Index Publication, *Museums and Galleries in Great Britain and Ireland*, listed alphabetically by place, with address, telephone number, how to get there by public transport, and many illustrations. Although the collection of each museum is given a few lines of description with special features noted, there are curious lapses.[1] London is, of course, fully covered in all the extraordinary variety of its collections. At 3s 6d this annual publication is a must. The companion guide from the same firm entitled *Historic Houses and Castles in Great Britain and Northern Ireland* will lead you to the many important paintings not in public museums and art galleries.[2]

The special exhibitions which museums and galleries, private and public, frequently mount are of obvious interest to the collector. They may well be the only opportunity of seeing privately owned paintings and, perhaps, what is more important, of making comparisons between different pictures. Exhibitions of an artist's work showing perhaps for the first time his full range and capabilities, can

[1] For example, of the National Museum of Wales: 'Comprises the Welsh National Museum of geology, botany, zoology, archaeology, industry and art.'

[2] My favourites are Waddesdon Manor, Petworth, and Wilton.

be a real eye-opener, leading to a reassessment of the painter's status and the values of his pictures.[1] Unfortunately, until there is a much publicized exhibition, some people show no interest in a great artist or group of artists, whose works are, in fact, on permanent display. How many of the thousands visiting the 1968 Royal Academy's Winter Exhibition of French eighteenth-century art, could hold a discussion about the same field as seen at the Wallace Collection, Manchester Square, London W1?[2] For readers living away from London, let me reiterate that I am merely citing examples and not suggesting that you must come to London to see French paintings (or any others for that matter). One of the finest landscapes by François Boucher (1703-70) I have ever seen is in the Bowes Museum, Barnard Castle, County Durham! Large scale exhibitions such as the 1968 one at the Royal Academy should not be allowed to overshadow smaller, more limited exhibitions, which can be of direct practical value to the collector. I am thinking especially of watercolour drawings which, as I have discussed, need very often to be sought out by the interested collector from their storage boxes in museums. For example, the exhibition at Kenwood in 1959 entitled 'William Gilpin and the Picturesque' was a unique opportunity to study the work of this family of artists. William's younger brother, Sawrey Gilpin (1733-1807)[3] was one of the

[1] I remember how enraptured I was, along with many others, by the superb French nineteenth-century paintings in the Arts Council Exhibition, 'Masterpieces of French Painting from the Bührle Collection', held at the National Gallery in 1961, but first shown in Edinburgh. One did not need much foresight then to realize that the rise in popularity and value of the Impressionists started in the 1950s, would be continued as strongly as ever in the 1960s, as indeed it has been. Emil Bührle is discussed among other world famous collectors, in a fascinating book, *The Great Collectors,* by Pierre Cabane.

[2] The finest collection of French eighteenth-century art outside France.

[3] Sawrey Gilpin collaborated with the landscape painter George Barret Senior (1732-84). See *The Victoria and Albert Museum Catalogue*, Figure 1.

most gifted animal painters of the eighteenth century, and a charming draughtsman.

A beginner who saw that exhibition and was prompted by it to acquire his own examples of Sawrey Gilpin's paintings and drawings of horses would today be very grateful to the organizers of the Exhibition for his initial introduction. The enthusiasm generated in the last five years for horse paintings of all kinds has resulted in a changed scale of values. None the less, the collector today might still be fortunate enough to acquire drawings by Gilpin. You will benefit by keeping *au fait* with these smaller exhibitions, particularly at the small Diploma Gallery[1] of the Royal Academy, the Arts Council in St James's Square, London, and Kenwood in Hampstead. Such exhibitions are frequently circulated in the provinces, and in any case many museums present similar displays. One of the advantages of seeing exhibitions may be the certainty of possessing a catalogue. These are usually reasonable in price and can be very useful for reference. Where no book has ever been written about the artist, and this is often the case, an exhibition catalogue may contain the most complete available information. Until the publication of his projected book, Mr Cyril Sorenson's excellent catalogue of the Brooking Exhibition held at the Bristol City Art Gallery in July 1966 remains the most authoritative writing on this very important artist.[2]

[1] The exhibition in 1962 of the Girtin family collection of drawings by Thomas Girtin was particularly memorable.

[2] Charles Brooking (1723-59) is the most oft-quoted example of the sudden realization of an artist's true worth, after being a minor figure for two centuries. In November 1963 at Christie's, a fine Brooking marine realized a record, far in excess of any previous figure, of 5,200 guineas. As very often happens, news of a record price 'flushes out' other examples from surprised owners. Within four months three Brookings were sold at Sotheby's for £15,500, £14,500, and £10,500; the level of values has been maintained.

I do realize that, to the beginner, the prospect of self-education by going to museums and exhibitions may be a little awesome. Although some people prefer to make their own way and reach their own conclusions about different artists' work, I think the majority would benefit from the programmes of lectures and instruction provided by museums about their collections. In the case of the National Gallery, for example, there are lunchtime lectures (1 p.m.) four days a week and special lectures for children at 2.30 p.m. By sending a stamped addressed envelope (3d stamp), a copy of the month's lecture programme will be sent to you. It is very worthwhile enquiring at any public gallery as to the educational facilities which are provided. At the same time, on your way in have a look at the publications counter. To take another example from the National Gallery, I think the beginner would find their 3s 6d publication, *Know the Gallery*, very good value.[1] As well as providing a summary guide to the Gallery with notes on each national school of painting, there are outstanding introductory sections, 'How Paintings are Done', 'Reasons for Painting', and a glossary of terms in common use. For those willing to pursue the subject more thoroughly, as indeed it deserves, the opportunities offered by local art societies, colleges of adult education, university extra-mural courses, are there for the taking.

No course, lecture, or guided tour can take the place of your private interest and familiarity with the paintings and drawings in a good public gallery. With apologies to those already aware, I would warn the beginner of two things. Firstly, if you are really looking at a gallery, as opposed to meandering through, you will find it tiring. In my experience, short repeated visits are more rewarding than a

[1] There are, of course, more elaborate guides, and a comprehensive choice of illustrations.

18 PETER LA CAVE (worked 1769–1810)
'Landscape with Figures and Watermill
Watercolour
Signed and dated 1801
Size: $7\frac{1}{4} \times 9\frac{3}{4}$ inches

19 FRANCIS NICHOLSON (1753–1844)
'Loch Lomond'
Watercolour
Signed and dated 1794 on mount, inscribed on reverse
Size: $11\frac{3}{4} \times 16\frac{1}{4}$ inches

20 FRANCIS NICHOLSON
'The Grass Market, Edinburgh'
Watercolour
Signed and dated 1807
Inscribed on reverse: 'From the corner of the Grass Market, Edinburgh, F. Nicholson 1807'
Size: $14\frac{1}{4} \times 20$ inches

21 DOMINIC SERRES (1722–93)
'Landscape with a Cottage beside a Wood'
Oil on canvas
Signed and dated 1762
Size: 12×14 inches

22 JULIUS CAESAR IBBETSON
(1759–1817)
'A View of Kilburn with London and St Paul's in the Distance'
Watercolour
Signed and dated 1787, and inscribed 'Kilburn'
Size: $10\frac{1}{2} \times 13$ inches

23 JULIUS CAESAR IBBETSON
'A View of Kilburn with London in the Distance'
Watercolour
Signed and dated 1787, and inscribed 'Kilburn'
Size: $10\frac{1}{2} \times 13$ inches

24 JULIUS CAESAR IBBETSON
'A View of Harrow from Kilburn'
Oil on canvas
Signed, inscribed and dated 1787
Size: 20 × 26 inches

25 PAUL SANDBY, RA
(1725–1809)
'Gathering Fuel in Windsor Great Park'
Watercolour
Size: 9½ × 12 inches

protracted stay. Incalculable harm is done to children who are marched around galleries long after they are bored and tired, thereby acquiring a lifelong horror of such places. Even the most devoted enthusiast can only absorb so much at a time, and in fact the more receptive you are the more tiring it may become. Never attempt any serious looking at paintings when you are hungry. Nothing is more certain to bring on 'museum fatigue', and waves of anti-cultural sentiments! Conversely, if you have an enjoyable and worthwhile visit, try to follow it according to the time of day, with a pleasant meal where you can discuss your impressions. I used to, and still do for that matter, spend a lot of small change on postcards of paintings I have seen. I enjoy confronting myself with snap selections from the huge box-full I have acquired, although it is a quiz better played with a friend. Allow three possible marks for each card, so that if you do not know the artist, you can be given one or two marks for recognizing the school and period. If this sounds rather childish, I can only say that tests of this kind only with real photographs, form part of university final examinations for those seeking a BA (Honours) degree in the History of Art!

An advanced form of this competition for those who pride themselves on their knowledge of the National Gallery, is provided by two books called *100 Details from Paintings in the National Gallery*, by Sir Kenneth Clark, published in 1938, and *More Details from Paintings in the National Gallery* by the same author, published a few years later.[1] The details are instructively placed, side by side in some cases, and the first book of details has a commentary. The illustrations are in black and white and the details are quite small in some cases, so recognition depends on spotting where the detail comes from – assuming you know the

[1] Both books are now out of print, but can be obtained from a library.

artist of the painting – or recognizing the detail through the style and technique. Incidentally, these close-up photographs are also useful for deducing date and school from technical details. For example, in *More Details*, page 84, there is a detail of a hand and forearm. You can see very clearly the grain of the English twill canvas, and the eighteenth-century *craquelure*. The execution looks rapid, rich, and sparkling. The answer is – a portrait of Queen Charlotte by Lawrence, painted in 1790.

I have emphasized the habitual aspect of museum-going because paintings become more, not less, rewarding with familiarity. The person who, after seeing a great painting, goes away saying, 'Well, I have seen it,' is like someone who has heard a Beethoven symphony for the very first time and sees no reason ever to repeat the experience.

It would be hard to think of clearer evidence of the tremendous rise in public interest in art, than the quantity of art books of all kinds now available. If you cannot readily visit museums and exhibitions in the way I have discussed, the quality of illustrations and text in many inexpensive art books would go a long way to compensate you. If you are a museum-goer, you have only to read one good book about an artist or school whose paintings you have seen in the original, to be for ever convinced of the value of reading. If, as in the last Chapter, having looked at the Earl of Bute by Reynolds, you then read the volume (31) devoted to him in the 'Masters' series, written by Keith Roberts, your appreciation of the artist and his work would be so much greater. The 'Masters' series, published weekly by Knowledge Publications, with each issue devoted to a single artist, has been on sale throughout the country. Contributors include many world authorities and the texts are all of a high standard. These essays on the artist are easily read, as they are only a few pages in length; in addition there is commentary on the plates. Although the quality of colour reproduction has perhaps been uneven, the 'Masters' do, in my opinion, represent very good value. The series has recently been completed in a hundred issues and these are available from: 'The Masters', Back Issues, 52 Poland Street, London W1. Numbers 1–65 cost 6s each, and 66 onwards 7s 6d each.

I could write many pages on the value available in art books today. Many of the leading publishers have brought out paperback series, like the 'Masters', on individual artists, but they have also systematically covered the whole history of art. In the same way, many museums abroad have been brought nearer home by lavishly illustrated volumes. At the same time, many larger hard-back books have been published, and many standard works revised and republished. With most publishers active in this way, the result is often that a beginner has a choice of books on a given subject ranging from pocket-sized paperbacks to a large, definitive study of an artist with a catalogue of all his known works. I have always found local libraries to be very helpful, not only in providing a good selection of art books, but in obtaining others on request.

The connection between reading and museum-going is obvious, but reading can also suggest interesting ways of arranging your visits to museums. I return to the National Gallery for convenience, to explain my meaning here. If, by reading, you learn that Rubens[1] was most influenced during his years in Italy by the great sixteenth-century Venetian artists, you would return to the museum, interested to compare a Titian or a Veronese with a Rubens. If, by reading from his journal[2] you know of Delacroix's

[1] *Recollections of Rubens*, by Jacob Burckhardt (Phaidon Press, first published 1950), price 10s 6d.

[2] *The Journal of Eugène Delacroix* (Phaidon Press, first published in 1951, but out of print).

fervent admiration and study of Rubens, you would have no trouble in tracing this influence in Delacroix's own work. By the same token, the landscapes of Richard Wilson (1713-82) possess the classical harmony of Claude Lorraine (1600-82), and the golden tones of Aelbert Cuyp (1620-91), the two artists whom Wilson most respected. Such influences are the medium which binds together the rich pigment of the history of art. It is more important to understand these broad developments than to crowd your head with too many detailed facts and biographical details. You might become aware of these connections from one school and century to another, by simply seeing the paintings of the artists I have mentioned, rather than reading about them. Yet you would still want to consult the books to confirm or confound what you had surmised. Certain artists are difficult to appreciate in any but a superficial way without some background knowledge of their lives. I am sure that the paintings of Van Gogh took on a new meaning for many people after the film about his life and work, starring Kirk Douglas.[1] The terrifying intensity of Van Gogh's personality shows in every swirling stroke of his art. Rembrandt's two self-portraits, executed at the age of thirty-four and in the last year of his life, draw the spectator to learn something of the story which they encompass.

Reading, like museums, may present the new collector with a problem of where to begin in the face of so many possibilities. Perhaps a general survey would summarize the whole range of art from which to select a field of special interest. No better survey exists than *The Story of Art*, by Professor Gombrich, published by Phaidon Press. That it is now in its eleventh revised edition, gives some idea of the success of this unique book. Equally renowned and indispensable is the *Dictionary of Art and Artists*, by Peter and

[1] Entitled, *Lust for Life*, it inevitably had a mixed critical reception.

Linda Murray, a Penguin reference book. Although the *Dictionary* has been published in greatly enlarged format with abundant illustrations, and at an appropriate price, I prefer it in its original red paperback edition at a cost of 7s 6d. Covering seven hundred artists, and defining artistic movements and technical terms, its special quality lies in the summary or assessment of each artist's style. It also lists the main museums where examples can be seen. A beginner's minimum 'survival kit' would be to have read carefully *The Story of Art*, and to have a copy of the *Dictionary* in his pocket!

Most of the artists whose works the beginner might hope to buy are obviously not to be found mentioned in these essentially general and introductory books. For detailed information, one must turn to the specialist books, whose value to the collector is immeasurable. The old saying in the art world that good books are the tools of the trade, is very apt. To find what information is available, and to consult many of the specialist books, one would ideally use an art library, such as the Victoria and Albert Museum Library.

I will limit myself to a few examples of books which are in everyday use. For dictionaries, the recently revised edition of Benezit,[1] in eight volumes, is a standard work of reference. If you speak German, you could use Thieme-Becker's *Dictionary*, the most complete ever, in thirty-six volumes. It is particularly useful for the references to other literature at the end of each entry, but as it took forty years to compile the early script is now outdated. If these languages are a problem, Bryan's *Dictionary of Painters and Engravers*, 5 vols. (Bell) is adequate and may be more helpful with English painters, although it badly needs revision. These straightforward dictionaries are more helpful than encyclopaedias[2]

[1] E. Benezit, *Dictionnaire des Peintres, Sculpteurs, Graveurs et Dessinateurs.* (It has not been translated, but the French is usually clear and simple.)

[2] Such as the recent *Encyclopaedia of World Art* (McGraw-Hill, 1960).

which do not, of necessity, include many lesser artists. For those interested in English painting, Professor Waterhouse's *Painting in England: 1530-1790*, in the Pelican History of Art, derives its particular value from the inclusion of smaller masters as well as many examples of the great names in English painting. The Paul Mellon Foundation for British Art is very generously promoting and organizing the study of English painting, so that the many gaps in the literature may be filled.

English landscape painting is the subject of the late Colonel M. H. Grant's indispensable eight-volume work, *The Old English Landscape Painters*.[1] A notable collector, Colonel Grant managed to compile a uniquely helpful book of reference, which is generously illustrated. A word of advice as to the use of this book may avoid misleading impressions. Colonel Grant wrote with a quaint wordiness to which one has to become accustomed. He held fairly strong personal convictions about certain artists, who may be given a rough passage without any evidence to support it, or be judged on the strength of one displeasing example the author has seen. None the less, the volumes are a remarkable achievement.

For those interested in Dutch painting, 1966 saw the publication of the long-awaited Pelican volume,[2] *Dutch Art and Architecture: 1600-1800* by Rosenberg, Slive, and Ter Kuile. A perfect example here of the difference between a book such as this, which is intended for the more demanding reader, and the purely specialist book on Dutch painters, is Walther Bernt's *Die Niederländischen Maler des 17 Jahrhun-*

[1] Published in exemplary style by Frank Lewis Publishers Ltd, Leigh-on-Sea, Essex.

[2] The 'Art and Architecture' volumes, which include *Painting in England*, already mentioned, are the most authoritative books of their kind. The volumes on Italy, France, Belgium, and *Painting in Europe: 1780-1880*, are specially relevant.

derts. This was originally published in three volumes, but now has a supplementary volume to fill the gaps and augment the initial work, and two further volumes on drawings, added by the same author. The fact that Bernt is not translated from the German, is less grave than might be imagined, because every artist listed, and it is unusual to find one who is not, is represented by one or more illustrations. What is specially useful in this book is the index where, after listing the illustrations of an artist, further references are given for other painters working under his influence. For instance, with Van Goyen, all his followers may be discovered by a careful use of this index. Alas, there are no comparable volumes of any kind which yield information about French or Italian lesser masters. If an industrious, systematic scholar would do for these schools what Bernt has done for the Dutch artists, the gratitude of English and American art historians, dealers and collectors, would be boundless. As it is, eighteenth-century French and Italian painters with the exceptions of Fragonard[1] and Canaletto[2] remain relatively unexplored and, above all, unillustrated in an up-to-date, efficient, format, despite the long-standing admiration of English collectors.

In the absence of individual books, specialized information is often to be found in articles in the many art magazines and journals, and exhibition catalogues to which I have already referred. Again, consulting them would involve using a suitably equipped library and, in many cases, knowing the name of the author, as there may be no index to periodical subject matter. I am thinking particularly of those occasions when you are reading a book, and, coming

[1] A definitive study of this master by Georges Wildenstein was published by the Phaidon Press in 1960.

[2] See W. G. Constable, *Canaletto: 1697-1768*, published by the Clarendon Press in 1962, in two volumes.

across a particularly interesting subject, you find a footnote which may read, 'For a full discussion of this interesting aspect, see Professor Smith's article in the *Burlington Magazine*, Volume X, January 1946.' I will give some examples of the value of periodicals in the next chapter.

The magazines which are perhaps most widely read are familiar, *The Connoisseur*, and *Apollo*. Published monthly, their advertising and exhibition reviews present an up-to-the-minute report on the availability of paintings, a record of saleroom events, and what is currently to be seen, in addition to good editorial articles and book reviews. The occasional purchase of *The Connoisseur* or *Apollo* is usually rewarding; they cost 12s 6d. If you could afford a subscription, so much the better, otherwise they are to be seen in most public libraries. *The Arts Review* is a fortnightly periodical, price 2s 6d, giving gallery reports with particular reference to contemporary painting in London and elsewhere. For those in London, the arts review inside the back cover, clearly sets out the programmes of lectures at the major public galleries.

Assuming you have the will and enthusiasm for museums and books, time may be a problem. I can think of a particular client of my firm, who, within a few years, has fitted in a great deal of museum and exhibition going, as well as reading in the evenings. His knowledge and therefore his skill and satisfaction as a collector are correspondingly enhanced. The time involved has not been taken at the expense of his very demanding job in the City, because if it were, he could hardly afford to remain an active collector. As he says, to escape into the world of painting from the strains and complexity of City finance, even for half an hour at lunchtime, is the most refreshing and heartening experience.

Some people, claiming to have no time for all this self-informing routine, spend hours vacuously wandering round junk shops and markets, which have been expertly sifted in advance. Therefore, the chances of discovering a great masterpiece are remote, and even if they were not how can one recognize a good painting without giving the eye and mind some training, or seeking professional help at least initially? Any collector will say that the best way to come to an understanding of paintings is through the daily contact which possession brings. In the end, ownership is even more important for you and your descendants than looking and reading about other people's acquisitions. To do both is the ideal.

3 How to Buy

Salerooms

In the introduction, I referred to something which everyone knows – that there has been a phenomenal increase in the publicity given to art and particularly to the art market. To the forefront are the quality Sunday newspapers, with the valuable help of their colour supplements, but the daily papers now give detailed coverage of many different events and personalities as never before. Without doubt, the lion's share belongs to the salerooms. Everyone is aware of the stature of Sotheby's and Christie's, and of the part they have played in establishing and maintaining London as the centre of the world's art business. Television has shown sales in progress and interviewed those in charge. Mr Peter Wilson has become familiar as the brilliant chairman of Sotheby's, the man who has led the firm to a dominant position both in London and New York – Sotheby's have amalgamated with Parke-Bernet Inc., the principal New York saleroom. Many factors underly the success of the salerooms. A lower selling commission,[1] duty-free entry and export of works of art, allied to greater professional ability, have brought paintings from all over the world for sale in London, closely followed by buyers, giving the salerooms their 'United Nations' atmosphere. Once this trend had become apparent, sellers

[1] Commission is only 10 per cent for pictures over £100, 12½ per cent for all others.

felt quite rightly that their paintings would do better in London, particularly old masters. The resultant earnings of foreign currency, particularly dollars, are impressive. Mr Wilson and his staff travel very extensively, as do Mr I. O. 'Peter' Chance and his staff at Christie's, to reassure these sellers that this is so and advise them on the sale of their collections.

Yet the increased volume of paintings come primarily from within the country. Detailed, daily newspaper reports of rising prices and records for artist's work are really the only publicity the salerooms need, and more effective than the most costly advertising campaign. Of course, it is effective both ways. Imagine a man, with a newspaper at breakfast, suddenly reading that a still life by Van Os has brought 19,000 guineas[1] at Christie's. He drops the paper, rushes to have a look at the name on that picture of fruit and flowers in the hall – 'Yes, by Jove! It is the same painter.' As his wife descends the stairs, he greets her with shining eyes, 'You know that picture your mother gave us, that I never really cared for – well, what do you think?', and another picture is on its way to London. To the buyer, on the other hand, news of even higher prices, confirms the wisdom of having bought, and continuing to buy good pictures – a topic to be discussed in due course. Reverting to the seller for a moment, don't think that the hypothetical instance I have given is far-fetched. On the contrary, there are countless people who, despite all the columns of newsprint, are far from knowing what they possess in the way of paintings. Every season[2] the reception counters of the salerooms are the scene of very agreeable surprises for those who have

[1] Jan Van Os (1744-1808), the record price for this artist's work established at Christie's, 23 July 1965.

[2] At Sotheby's and Christie's sales are usually held from early October until the end of July.

unknowingly brought in what turn out to be valuable paintings. Even more exciting are the occasions when pictures pass from unsuspecting owners to unsuspecting auctioneers, and are only discovered during viewing immediately before the sale. Of the many well-reported instances, my favourite is of the zebra that turned up at Harrods.

However celebrated this great institution in Knightsbridge, Harrods themselves would not, I am sure, think of their fortnightly furniture and household effects sales as major events of the London saleroom season. Imagine then the surprise one autumn day in 1960 when rumours spread to the West End that a genuine painting by George Stubbs (1724-1806), our greatest animal painter, was hanging on view at Harrods Auction Rooms. Everyone made his way there and was duly greeted by a remarkable painting known as the 'Princess Charlotte's Zebra'. This creature had been brought from South Africa, the first zebra seen in England, and presented to George III, when Prince of Wales, and Princess Charlotte. Stubbs painted the picture not as a Royal Commission, but from his interest in the zebra and for his own satisfaction in depicting it. Both the painting, which was exhibited in the artist's lifetime, and the circumstances surrounding its creation, were well recorded, but its whereabouts had for some years been a mystery. At the sale on 19 October 1960, Stubbs' zebra was sold for £20,000. Its last previous appearance at auction had been at Christie's in 1923 when it fetched £220 10s.[1] The painting is now in the collection of Mr and Mrs Paul Mellon.

Most of all, the newspapers relish stories of pictures discovered in salerooms, because they are rarer and often do not become public knowledge. I think it reflects great credit on a buyer's knowledge if he alone can spot what a

[1] See G. Reitlinger, *The Economics of Taste* (Barrie & Rockliffe, 1961).

picture really is when everyone has had the same opportunity of doing so. This is a viewpoint rarely shared by those who 'missed' the picture.

To the mixture of success, romance, mystery and money, another ingredient has been carefully added. In the decade since Sotheby's held the first after-dinner, evening-dress, social event type of sale, the salerooms have almost gained a place on the social calendar. Today, you can look round during a sale and see how potential buyers are outnumbered by interested non-buying spectators. Among them are the intense catalogue markers, those who watch only the pictures one after another on the rostrum, and those who mainly watch other people. For that tedious gap, on a wet morning between coffee and lunch, the salerooms appear to be the answer. Sotheby's and Christie's have been obliged to restrict the attendance by having every seat ticketed for important sales. Even so, the 'audience' has overflowed out of the actual auction room to side rooms, to follow the sale on closed-circuit television. Big sales have an atmosphere which is undeniably intriguing but difficult to analyse. Emotions are heightened by being suppressed, because sales in London are conducted quietly with a kind of nonchalant decorum.[1] Problems of accommodation do not arise at the less important sales which make up the large majority of the season's business. The public tend to imagine that every lot brings a major financial clash with bidding at £10,000 a nod. On the contrary, the majority of paintings and drawings sold go for less than £100.

All things considered, the salerooms seem very inviting to the collector – maybe he will make a discovery, and even if he doesn't, there are thousands of pictures in a price range he can afford, and anyway, everyone seems to go to

[1] Momentarily ruffled by the now celebrated dispute over the sale of Rembrandt's portrait of Titus at Christie's in March 1965.

sales. Picture buying in the salerooms is an adventure. Whether it is a happy adventure or not will depend on your knowledge and know-how.

The first thing to understand about picture sales at Sotheby's and Christie's, for example, is the cataloguing system.[1] On the face of it, the catalogue is puzzling. You will see a landscape in greys and browns catalogued as, 'Goyen, oil on panel', and so on. At first glance, it certainly has the colouring and style of the great Dutch painter, but when you look at the back of the panel, you will find that the wood is a reddy-brown mahogany. Aware, as you are, that most seventeeth-century Dutch painters worked on oak panels, you begin to have doubts about the age of the picture. Turning to the paint surfaces again, you see that it has not the characteristic appearance of a seventeenth-century picture, which has been discussed. You quite rightly decide that the landscape cannot really be by Van Goyen, because it looks like an eighteenth or nineteenth-century picture. Why then does the catalogue say 'Goyen?' The explanation is simple, but you must always keep it in mind when using the catalogue. If, in the opinion of the saleroom the painting is the genuine work of Van Goyen it would be catalogued with the artist's full Christian and surname – Jan Van Goyen. If they doubt that it is actually by Van Goyen, but feel that it comes from his circle or studio, it would be catalogued with the artist's initial and surname – J. Van Goyen. Alternatively, if they know it is *not* by Van Goyen nor even from his immediate circle, but loosely 'in the manner of' or 'after' his work, it will be catalogued with the artist's surname only. Thus, the picture you have examined was painted a hundred years after Van Goyen's death, but whoever painted it did so in the style of Van Goyen, and the picture is catalogued 'Goyen' because it is in the manner

[1] Used in most other picture salerooms.

of or, in the case of a copy after a known work, 'after' this master.

Another important detail of the cataloguing system is the distinction between 'signed' and 'bears signature', 'dated' and 'bears date'. The word 'bears' implies real doubt as to the authenticity of either signature or a date, and is quite distinct from a picture being described as 'signed and dated'. As always, although the catalogue may read clearly 'signed and dated', this is an opinion not a guarantee.[1] Incidentally, you would be well advised to look carefully at any paintings of this kind which appear eighteenth century and have an English feel to them. Dutch landscape painters of the seventeenth century had a strong influence on eighteenth-century English painters, many of whom copied Ruisdael and Van Goyen in their student years, notably Gainsborough. In the nineteenth century too, painters of the Norwich school studied the Dutchmen, in particular Aelbert Cuyp (1620-91). If you were able to find an early Gainsborough, say, catalogued as 'Ruisdael' or 'Goyen', you need no longer call yourself a beginner! To give another example of the cataloguing system with an English painter – Joseph Mallord William Turner, RA, J. M. W. Turner, Turner. The frequency with which Turner's name appears in all three categories reflects not only the vastness and complexity of Turner's actual work, but the extent of his contemporary and later copyists and imitators. The same is true of many major artists. They are the artists who brought something new to painting and changed the course of its development.

Their style is highly personal, with strongly pronounced characteristics, which could be easily copied. At the same

[1] During the preparation of this Chapter, the salerooms have now, in many cases, provided these details of their cataloguing system in the front of their catalogues.

time, other artists could follow their example without losing their own identities. They interpreted the achievements of the great artist in their own way. You must make a clear distinction between the work of an imitator, pure and simple, and a genuine follower. In doing so, don't make the common mistake of calling paintings by contemporary or later imitators, like the imaginary Van Goyen you examined, fakes. Ninety-nine per cent of these pictures were not painted to deceive anyone, no more than the painters of today who copy pictures in the National Gallery would think of their efforts as fakes or forgeries, as I have already mentioned. Painters of the nineteenth and twentieth centuries are much easier to fake, but even faked pictures of this kind are rarely seen, despite the ballyhoo which surrounds them. Faked Corots are the most renowned, especially in the United States.

To summarize, you will frequently see pictures in the sales which are not by the great artist but contemporary with him, and by his immediate pupils; these are called 'school pictures'. You will see all manner of pictures, good and bad, which are like the artist's work but later in date, these are called simply, 'late copies' or 'late pictures'. You will seldom see a real fake, if that is not too contradictory.

For most buyers, identifying the work of the so-called minor artists is really the crux of the question. The genuine work of the major artists is appearing less in the salerooms and when it does, only the wealthier collector can bid for it. With the increasing scarcity of good paintings in general, the buyer finds himself in the situation of a prospector working a somewhat impoverished mine. He must shift a lot of 'waste' material to find something of value. As we have seen, the catalogue will help but it is by no means infallible. If you say to yourself, 'I will be on the safe side and only go for paintings catalogued with the artist's full

26 PAUL SANDBY, RA
'View of Cory-lin on the Upper Clyde'
Gouache
Signed
Size: 12½ × 17½ inches

27 PAUL SANDBY, RA
'Pembroke Castle from the West'
Oil on panel,
Inscribed on reverse
Size: 12 × 18¾ inches

28 THOMAS ROWLANDSON (1756–1827)
'Travellers on Bodmin Moor'
Watercolour, pen and ink
Size $6\frac{3}{4} \times 9\frac{1}{2}$ inches

29 CHARLES TOWNE (1763–1840)
'Landscape with Figures, Horses and Sheep'
Oil on canvas,
Signed with monogram
Size: 24 × 31½ inches

30 JOHN SELL COTMAN (1782–1842)
'Leatherhead Church'
Watercolour
Signed and dated 1800, and inscribed on reverse
Size: 14¼ × 21 inches

name,' you must immediately turn to the front of your catalogue and read the conditions of sale. There can be no doubt what they say: 'They act as agents only and are not responsible for the correct description, genuineness, nor authenticity of, nor any fault nor defect, in any lot, and *make no warranty whatsoever*'. The old adage, 'buyer beware', remains the guiding principle. Too often people use their catalogues without understanding the way in which they are compiled and that the information it gives is only an opinion, offering no guarantee of any kind.[1]

One other point about reading a catalogue is worth mentioning. Pictures have often acquired an impressive record which is printed in the catalogue. Several well-known collections are listed, together with records of exhibitions and mentions in the appropriate books. Normally, this is a good sign, but remember that it can be meaningless if the picture is not by the artist. Occasionally, provenances have become attached to the wrong picture, and obviously this can be disastrous. Don't let a dazzling pedigree prevent you from looking at the picture as closely as ever. A good general tip when viewing sales is to look at the picture first and decide what you think it is. Then look at the number and see what the catalogue says. In this way, you will increase your ability to recognize different artist's work. You will see pictures by artists whose work is not easily seen in public galleries, and, what is equally instructive, you will see pictures which are near misses for an artist's work – and these you rarely see in public collections!

Unfortunately for the inexperienced buyer, there is one outstanding difference between a saleroom and a public gallery. Imagine you were walking round the National Gallery deciding what pictures were the soundest to buy. You can see the pictures clearly because, with some excep-

[1] Conditions of sale now printed in the catalogue.

tions, they are cleaned. Remembering the importance of condition, you can look in the Gallery catalogue which will tell you what the state of preservation is, if you cannot see for yourself. Of authenticity, you need have no doubt. Contrast this happy situation with walking round the viewing of a sale of pictures. In a picture sale, you will find that very often the interesting pictures are those in an undisturbed state. Indeed, the salerooms encourage owners to send their paintings for sale undisturbed in every way, because they know that the buyer's interest is so much greater when a painting cannot be seen clearly. Potential buyers might read into it much more than is really there beneath the grime and so pay a higher price. In any case, if a picture is hanging at a sale freshly cleaned, re-varnished, and even re-framed, it poses obvious problems. Could it be that it is in a poor state and has been done up to disguise the fact, or has it recently been on the market? If it has been on the market and a dealer could not sell it, there must be a valid reason. On the other hand, if the painting has been sent in by private owners, who obviously have bought it recently, why are they selling? Again, this causes disquiet.

How difficult then for the beginner to recognize an artist's work when it is obscured by dirty varnish and grime. Let us assume that there is no doubt as to the artist of an uncleaned picture, but it remains to judge its quality in order to decide if it is a first-class example of his work or a mediocre example.

If I had to confine myself to offering one piece of advice only to the collector, it would be that whatever artist holds your interest, try to buy the best possible example of his work. It is much better to have a really excellent example of a minor master than a poor picture by a greater name. Collectors tend to be drawn by names and buy the name rather than the picture – a practice which can lead to a very disappointing houseful of pictures. If you know roughly the value of an artist's work, and you know you cannot afford it, try to buy a good watercolour or drawing by the artist, rather than a painting. If the good watercolours and drawings are too costly, then you must lower your sights to another artist and plump for his best until you can afford the more important artist's work.

We tend to forget that artists had to earn their livings first and foremost, and to do this they had to paint pictures. Obviously, some of these pictures have the inspiration, or whatever you care to call it, of an artist, while others are the products of a man earning his living – the familiar 'pot-boilers'. I think this applies particularly to those nineteenth-century artists who were so much in demand in their own lifetimes – success can lead to 'pot-boiling' in a different way. Even great artists have lapses of a kind.

With an artist whose work maintains a consistently high standard of quality, the choice between one picture or another may depend solely on condition. As I have said, the catalogue of the sale offers no help here. The pitfalls are fairly obvious. A picture may seem perfectly desirable in subject, size, and price range, but what if the paint surface is worn, or the priming loosened, or the canvas or panel in a poor way, or any of the other defects which may be hidden by the dirt? I have already talked about a picture which has fairly obviously been 'done up' for sale, but this might be the least of the stumbling blocks. Suppose that an eighteenth-century painting had been overcleaned in 1850, but remained untouched since. A hundred years of accumulated dirt could easily make it look in an original condition, and you must therefore look at it very closely. In the same way, an early eighteenth-century picture might have been in a distressed state by the early nineteenth century, but then very carefully and skilfully restored and left undisturbed after that. The old restoration has long since settled in and, again, there is well over a century of natural dirt through which to peer. Alternatively, the defects of a picture might have been discovered much more recently, and it has been artificially dirtied down or 'toned' to avoid it looking recently cleaned in the way I mentioned.

The serious saleroom buyer can obtain helpful advice from the saleroom experts, apart from the routine estimate or anticipated price which is freely available to everyone. Remember that such advice will still be subject to those same 'conditions of sale', and that when the hammer falls it will be your money which is being spent and you must accept any risks involved, just as bargains will be entirely to your credit.

Picture Dealers

The alternative to buying for yourself in salerooms is to buy from an art dealer. This guide would be woefully incomplete without discussing the role of the picture dealer, whom I have called the professional collector. As a picture dealer myself, the son of a picture dealer, and brought up to be a picture dealer, I would not want to miss the opportunity of writing about a job which I enjoy so much.

I am tempted to say that as a profession it is immensely varied in pictures, people, and places; exciting, unpredictable, satisfying. But there are some other jobs of which the same can be said. Where I feel picture dealing is most intriguing is in the degree of personal involvement. For, like all serious dealers in old and beautiful things, picture dealers are not really effective either as buyers or sellers unless they themselves feel something for the picture. I will not put it more strongly than that. Picture dealing is not a nine to five job, but rather a way of life, at once a business, an interest, and a hobby. It is absorbing.

Good art dealers rely first and foremost on their reputation and good standing in an extremely competitive business. Reputation is, in effect, the sustained quality and worth of the pictures they buy and above all, offer for sale, and their fairness in doing so. There are, of course, bad art dealers like there are bad barristers, builders, and brokers, whose faults are probably those of ignorance rather than guile. Inevitably, there must be those who try and exploit the enormous public interest in buying pictures. Like the ill-informed collector, their day is past.

To be successful, the picture dealer must combine so far as possible, the functions of an art historian, a good financier, an investment adviser, a student of human nature, and a public relations officer.

What should the beginner's approach be? With the exception of one or two of the largest firms, picture galleries are relatively small, personal businesses, where an art dealer's individual taste is reflected in the kind of picture he buys. The beginner would therefore, be well advised to look around the galleries before deciding what sort of pictures hold his interest. Another factor in your choice of art dealer is very important – he should be someone whom you come to like. Picture collecting should be fun, and you cannot work happily at it with someone or their firm whom you do not get along with. A good recommendation can be a great help at this stage, but it should come from someone with personal experience of the firm recommended, and you should see the purchases on which it is based. If the person recommending has had a long experience of the gallery, time will have shown that he was well advised.

In making your choice, reflect that the best galleries are not necessarily those with the most elaborate premises or the widest advertising. Indeed, one of the most important picture dealers in London has a modest-sized gallery, does not hold exhibitions, and does virtually no advertising.

You should be well received in any gallery and welcome to come on exploratory visits without feeling that you must purchase. If you like the gallery, and you have seen some of their pictures and asked the prices, but you have not found what you want, talk to the principal or one of his assistants. Tell him what you want, and if it is an artist or field with a wide variation in price, give some guidance as to what you are willing to spend. A good art dealer will make a note of what you have told him, and let you know when he has the right kind of painting to offer. If you are too cagey and evasive, he probably will not. With the scarcity of pictures, you may have to be patient, but a good picture is well worth waiting for. Meanwhile, do look at other pictures which pass through the gallery's hands, even if they are outside your tastes and resources. Some collectors feel that if they call on a dealer and look at pictures, they ought to buy. This is a mistake and one which may prevent your learning a good deal by seeing different kinds and categories of pictures. Most picture dealers are pleased to show exceptional pictures, especially to beginners who may learn most from seeing them. You may not possess a hundredth part of the price of the picture, but you are training your eye and broadening your tastes by seeing it. You may one day make enough money to afford such pictures, and when you do, you will have the advantage of knowing what you want. This possibility is not lost on the dealer who must hope that among today's beginners are tomorrow's major clients.

Having consulted a professional, you must, allowing for your own inclinations, be guided by what he says in respect of quality and real desirability. Generally speaking, paintings of whatever variety are basically good and worthwhile or they are not – and this is not a question of opinion, taste, or fancy. Those beginners who use the ever popular phrase, 'I don't know anything about pictures, but I know what I like,' must remember the first half of the sentence as much as the second half. In other words, if, by your own admission, you do not know anything about pictures, try not to be too hasty in deciding which ones you like or dislike. Pictures grow on you, as they say, so give them a chance to do so. When you are more or less decided on a picture, it may be a good idea to have it at your home for a few days to see it in its future surroundings, and to be absolutely certain of your decision one way or the other. Most dealers are quite agreeable to picture hanging on approval for a short time. Naturally, they may want some form of security on the first occasion. It is much better to take a little time before you buy, than to come back later and say you want to change the picture because you are not happy with it – picture dealers will try to help you, but they are not running lending libraries. Different firms have different practices in respect of taking pictures back, and you should ask about this when you buy. Good dealers will vouch for the authenticity of their pictures.

The recurring thought of many collectors with their first purchases from a dealer, is whether they are paying a fair price. Obviously, this is a difficult subject, because the price of an artist's work cannot be quoted like a stock or share. You do not pick up the newspaper and see that Richard Wilson is up two points, or that Picasso yesterday, after early buying, fell back towards the close, to finish one-and-six down. The range in price between a given artist's lesser pictures and his few very best or single outstanding picture, can be considerable, but none the less, there is within the range, a correct price for a picture. The price therefore, depends on assessing the status of the picture within the artist's work, and so placing it in the appropriate position in the price range. Valuation is an individual matter, and varies as much as individuals. Every auction sale of pictures is a form of valuation. Bidders drop out when the bidding passes what, in their opinion (or valuation) the picture is worth. One cannot dismiss this point by saying that it is a question of differing resources. I have often seen five or six dealers of equal purchasing power drop out at five different figures. In the same way, prices vary to some extent according to a dealer's individual judgment. What should the attitude of the beginner be?

Firstly, he should remember what I have already mentioned, that a well-established dealer relies on his reputation, and a good reputation is not built by overcharging for pictures. If this is not a satisfactory logic, you can take a second opinion. Alternatively, the record of sale prices, *Art Prices Current*, can be consulted at a library. However, this annual publication, like so much of statistics, can be very deceptive. For example, a picture comparable to the one under consideration may not have appeared for some years to give a comparison.[1] Being simply a record of sale catalogues, this book is not selective and many examples cited were not necessarily genuine, and brought low prices, giving a misleading value of the artists' work. Initially, there must be an element of trust on the part of the beginner that he is being charged the right price. In the great majority of cases, this trust would not be misplaced, and for the remainder a combination of caution and knowledge are the best safeguards. If you have become the customer of a particular dealer and are pleased in every respect with what you have bought, you need not feel barred from buying from another dealer or a saleroom. This is obviously your

[1] Even dealers suffer from the same problem in a rapidly changing market, and sometimes undersell.

31 JOHN CONSTABLE (1776–1837)
'At Buckden, Yorks.'
Watercolour
Inscribed and dated 1832
Size: $5\frac{7}{8} \times 8\frac{3}{4}$ *inches*

32 JOHN RUSSELL (1744–1806)
'Portrait of a Young Girl in a Red Cloak'
Pastel
Size: 21½ × 15½ inches

33 SIR MARTIN ARCHER SHEE (1769–1850)
'Portrait of Captain Edward Becher'
Oil on canvas
Size: 30 × 25 inches

34 JOHN DOWNMAN, RA (1750–1824)
'Portrait of Mrs Mary Seawell of Great Bookham'
Watercolour
Oval, signed and dated 1792
Size: 8 × 6¾ inches

decision, but you would be wise to ask if your 'own' dealer will advise you, particularly when you want to buy in sales. A policy of loyalty, assuming everything is satisfactory, will show dividends in the end. First-class pictures are scarcer than buyers, and the steady customer is given priority.

I have assumed throughout this discussion of price that pictures are sold in galleries at their present-day market value, regardless of what they cost to buy. I mention this because beginners tend to think, again in commodity terms, of a wholesale buying price, to which a retailer's profit is added. This is only part of the story. Some beginners, embarking on their first purchase, spend a lot of time exercising their mind as to what the dealer's profit might be – this is pure guesswork and unproductive. He may be selling it on a ten per cent commission basis for a private owner, he may have bought it in a sale and be charging a fifty per cent profit, he may have bought it in a sale where it was only partially seen for what it was, and so had a hundred per cent profit, he may have bought it in a remote junk shop for a fraction of its true value, and his profit may be several hundred per cent. Whatever the profit margin, when averaged out – and it will not be different, in most cases, from many other professional jobs – it must be put against the fact that no dealer is completely infallible. There is a degree of risk in the buying of any picture. As we have seen earlier in this chapter, an unseen flaw in the condition of a picture can be very detrimental. An adverse report from an authority on the authenticity of a picture, bought with complete confidence, will mean demotion and a loss. Decisions have sometimes to be very quick unless the dealer wants to risk losing the opportunity of buying.

Apart from these admittedly uncommon contingencies, profit margins have to be put against the more obvious running expenses. To acquire, prepare and maintain premises in the right situation and to employ competent staff, are basic problems. To pay the charges of expert re-liners, restorers, frame makers, photographers, advertisers, shippers, are essentials, as are time and money spent in research. These are not the cares of the collector, but ones he should appreciate. In truth, picture dealers find their satisfaction in the growth and splendour of collections which have been formed with their help, and this is most collections. A not particularly sensible person asked me why I was writing this book, when, as a dealer myself, I might give away trade secrets and tell the customers too much. But it is very much easier to sell paintings to knowledgeable and appreciative collectors, because they recognize quality in a picture when they see it. Beginners can learn a great deal from an art dealer and the more informed the beginners are, the more intelligent their interest, and thus the more they learn.

This chapter on how to buy is briefly summarized. However and wherever you buy, never let it be lost to view that the picture is the important factor. Authenticity, quality and good condition must be the guiding principles. Any collector knows that the best examples are the most sought after, and in a sharply rising market you must be prepared to pay a high price for the best. It is, in my opinion, advisable to concentrate available resources into one first-class picture or drawing, rather than several of secondary importance. There is no doubt that this approach holds the greatest investment potential.[1]

Never lament too long over any mistakes you make, but rather cut your losses and buy again. Experience is experience. Above all, collecting should be enjoyable.

[1] See Chapter 5 on investment.

4 What to Buy

In the introduction, I stated that a beginner's choice of what to collect will be a matter for his personal taste. It would be tempting to shelter, as other authors on this subject have done, behind this remark to avoid making definite suggestions with specific examples. Rather than produce an inconclusive survey of the many possibilities open to the beginner, I have preferred a narrower but more informative discussion of selected artists, within reach. Naturally, a degree of personal choice enters such selection, but remember that I am not making suggestions based entirely on my own preferences. The examples illustrated have been bought by private collectors of widely differing backgrounds and tastes. It goes without saying that these items would not have been offered for sale if they did not also represent good assets for the future, nor in most cases would they have been purchased if this were not so. You will find several omissions, because I have tried to concentrate on less obvious spheres of interest, in terms of artist and subject matter, which have potential. Thus, however reluctantly, there is no mention of *genre* or conversation pictures, Venetian subjects, important English artists like Augustus John, sporting paintings, and other very popular fields.

I have devoted much attention to watercolours because the art of watercolour, though not originated, was developed, perfected and sustained by the English watercolour school, in a manner without parallel in the history of painting. Of the limited instances where English artists could fairly claim to have surpassed their Continental contemporaries, watercolour painting is the most conspicuous.

Watercolour was mainly used in its pure form by English artists, where water is the medium for the ground pigments. To the water must be added a small quantity of gum as a binding material, in the same way that inks needs a binder to make them adhere to paper. The gum commonly used was gum arabic from the acacia plant. To keep the colour moist, especially when tubes were introduced, glycerine was used, but this is an additive and not an essential ingredient.[1] In pure watercolour painting, colours are either transparent or semi-transparent and derive their light from the whiteness of the paper in the way that oil painters may employ a transparent glaze over a light priming. For the watercolourist, white is provided by the paper, for there is no pigment.[2] The paper may be left showing for maximum highlight or covered with transparent washes, but it should never be obscured or lost. Once a colour has been put onto the paper, it may be modified by another wash, but it can never be lightened because each successive wash, of whatever colour, further hides the paper which is the source of lightness. To remove or lighten a wash of colour the painter must dissolve it with water on his brush and dab it off with a rag or sponge. Most watercolour painters worked over a preliminary drawing in ink, pencil, chalk, or charcoal, which played a varying role in the finished picture. Hence the term 'watercolour drawing'. You will have no difficulty in distinguishing between a pen and ink drawing to which

[1] Honey was also used as an additive to overcome brittleness in the gum when dry.

[2] When white opaque pigment is added to watercolour the medium is known as bodycolour or gouache. See below under Paul Sandby.

watercolour has been added, almost in a secondary role, compared to an example where a faint pencil preparation has been almost entirely hidden by the colour, or erased after it is dry. Only faint pencil work can be eliminated, for in the other mediums the drawing remains very much a part of the completed picture. Earlier practitioners normally worked over a sound pen and ink drawing to which was sometimes added faint washes in the same monochrome ink.

The subtleties of technique, from the fine stipple effects of the point of the brush to the broad sweep of a 'drag' stroke or the 'floating in' of a broad wash, rival in every respect the skills of the painter in oils. To the layman, the infinite gradations in the strength of a colour are so fine, particularly in a sky as it lightens towards the horizon, that you need to look at a watercolour carefully and with understanding, to appreciate the skill of the painter.

As with oil paintings, you may seek help in recognition by the physical 'clues'. Eighteenth-century drawings are usually done on hand-made paper which is thin and distinguishable in texture from the heavier machine-made paper of the nineteenth century. With the more solid papers, later artists could take out or modify colours by washing over and rubbing out, as described, much more readily. Stouter paper also permitted the technique of scraping off the colour with a blade or the wooden tip of the brush to expose the paper and so create a highlight.[1] As the earlier and thinner papers would not permit these practices, their presence can be a useful indication of period.

Fugitive colours, especially blues in watercolour, react to prolonged exposure to strong daylight, and bad fading is often the cause of a drawing's rejection. The collector of old watercolour drawings must be prepared to accept a

[1] Turner was notably effective with 'scraping out'.

degree of fading as a natural consequence of age. Happily, the traditional practice of keeping watercolours in portfolios[1] away from light and damp, means that examples will often be found that are in a pristine condition.

The brown spots, called foxing or spotting, which mar watercolours, can often be removed by an expert restorer. Non-professional attempts to remove dirt or spotting from a drawing result in a bleached spot or an overall effect more detrimental to the drawing's appearance than the original defect. Discolouration may be caused by impurities in the rags from which the paper was made or by the action of damp or insects. Sometimes, watercolours have been framed without proper mounts and the resins in the wood of the backboards seep through and discolour the paper. Watercolours that have been overcleaned have a scrubbed look which leaves certain colours strong and others very weak, destroying the balance and delicate harmony which are the very essence of a watercolour's charm.

The study of both the technique and development of English watercolour painting has greatly benefited from the recent publication of the first two volumes of the late Martin Hardie's *Watercolour Painting in Britain*.[2] This is not only a work of immense scholarship, which brings together information from the writings of all important authorities, but one whose superb production compliments the attractiveness of the subject. Instead of attempting to reproduce the subtle colours of the medium, illustrations are in very fine black and white matt photographs, of which there are over 240 in the first volume.

At the other end of the scale, you will find the V. & A.'s illustrated booklet No. 4, *British Watercolours* by Grahame Reynolds, HMSO, price 3s, a useful short introduction

[1] These should be properly made drawing boxes, specially for the purpose.

[2] Published by Batsford, 1966-7, at 6 gns. each.

with forty illustrations from the Museum's collection. There are, of course, many other books on the subject but of these, the important ones are out of print. Until the publication of Hardie, one of the most often quoted sources of information was *Early English Watercolours* by Iolo Williams, published in 1952, nor indeed is it superseded by the more recent book. However, it may only be seen in specialist libraries because the printers' blocks were destroyed and it is now a very rare book. Those who bought Iolo Williams' book in 1952 for a few guineas have been rewarded for their interest, as it were, for a copy is now worth sixty or seventy pounds. As I have mentioned, detailed writings are mainly to be found in magazines and journals, and I will give examples for the artists illustrated. One unusual book, for those who read French, is *Le Paysage Anglais à L'Aquarelle, 1760-1851* by Henri Lemaître, published by Bordas, Paris 1955. Although rather vague in places and inclined to be very wordy, this French writer gives a very perceptive commentary on the development as a whole, and his remarks about Paul Sandby are particularly good. The keen collector will soon be provided with an exhaustive reading list because the third and concluding volume of Martin Hardie's work is to include a full bibliography.

Many collectors keep their watercolours in boxes, mounted but unframed. The majority do so either as a permanent safeguard against fading or more probably because their wall space is taken by oil paintings. If you are not yet so fortunate, display your watercolours and let them take the role normally played by paintings. Watercolours predominate in my own home, and I have found it successful to frame them, with a narrow margin of mount showing, not in conventional drawing frames, but in narrow picture frames which would in the ordinary way be used for oil paintings. To my taste this has a very satisfactory effect and seems to accord to the watercolours the importance which they deserve. To find the equivalent degree of artistic skill and quality in an oil painting would be a difficult undertaking, even with considerable resources. Having my watercolours permanently hanging, I have kept a vigilant eye for any sign of fading, and this has not taken place. Whether and how you frame your watercolours is naturally a matter of choice, but they must be mounted, and it is worth extra expense to ensure a really well-chosen and well-made mount. Good mount makers have a marvellous selection of papers available, and can put in perfect wash-line borders where they are wanted. Drawings are held into their mounts with two small hinges under the upper edge, and allowed to hang free. As with stamps in an album, hinges should always be used and drawings must never be stuck down on to the back of the mount, as this may ruin them. Perhaps, at some time in the past, a badly measured mount has been made for a drawing, or a mount from another drawing of nearly the same size used, and you may find part of the drawing covered. A proper mount should 'catch' only the very edge of the drawing and no more. Lift the mount to make sure it fits and is not, for example, covering the quarter of an inch at the bottom where the artist put his signature.

By focusing your attention on watercolours, especially early English watercolours, I am not, of course, making a novel proposition. Indeed, it is a traditional form of collecting in England, as witness the great personal bequests to the V. & A. However, since certain categories of paintings have ceased to be within the smaller collector's reach, there has been a greatly accelerated interest in watercolours. The legacy of this attitude of regarding them as substitutes lingers on in the erroneous belief that they should be very much less costly than oil paintings. Traditionally, the prefix 'early English' related to the masters of the eighteenth

35 GEORGE CHAMBERS (1803–40)
'Bleak House, Broadstairs'
Oil on artist's millboard
Signed
Size: 11 × 18 inches

36 JAMES HOLLAND (1800–70)
'A View of Margate'
Watercolour
Inscribed and dated 23 September 1861
Size 4 × 6 inches

37 JAMES BAKER PYNE (1800–70),
'The Post-town of Luino, Lago Maggiore'
Oil on canvas
Signed and dated 1869, and numbered No. 726
Size: 26¼ × 39½ inches

38 JAMES WILSON CARMICHAEL (1800–68)
'Shipping off Portsmouth'
Oil on canvas
Signed and dated 1863
Size: 24 × 39 inches

39 JAMES WILSON CARMICHAEL,
'A View of Durham'
Oil on artist's millboard
Signed
Size: 9 × 13 inches

40 DAVID ROBERTS, RA (1796–1864)
'The Priory of Pluscardine, Morayshire'
Watercolour
Signed, inscribed and dated 12 September 1848
Size 9½ × 13½ inches

century, or earlier in a few cases, and the early nineteenth century. Many people, myself among them, regard this period as the most desirable in the way that one might prefer a Georgian or Regency house to a Victorian one. The present rise in the prices of Victorian paintings may, in some cases, have as much to do with the scarcity of eighteenth-century examples, as with their intrinsic merits. Clearly, the nineteenth century offers many attractive possibilities in paintings and watercolours, but the degree of selectivity may need to be greater. It is a simple fact of history that, with the obvious exception of Turner, the English school of the mid and later nineteenth century does not have the stature of the corresponding period in the eighteenth century.

In making my selection, I have followed my own advice to you in the 'How to Buy' Chapter. Firstly, authenticity is established, wherever appropriate, by signature. In doing so, I have not, however, rejected an unsigned example if it is better and more suitable than a signed one. As you know, no rules, or virtually none, govern whether an artist consistently signed his work or not. A painter already discussed, Jan Van Goyen, is one of the few artists whose genuine paintings are signed. At least, I have never seen one that was not.

As to quality, there seems little point in setting mediocre standards when these are precisely what I am urging you to avoid. My hope is that the illustrations may serve as a measure of quality and, because of their variety, of comparative value – both for different examples of the artists discussed, and for the work of others who are related but not included. In any case, it would be misleading for many of the painters to be represented by anything but their best work. Because of the great importance I attach to condition, only those paintings and watercolours were eligible that could not be faulted in this respect. This is especially important for watercolours. Fading, beyond a minimal acceptable amount, is ruled out. The standard of quality and condition has been set with my other piece of buying advice in mind, namely, the acquisition of one first-class work, rather than several lesser things. Although this calls for restraint and patience on the part of the buyer, it is wisest in the long run. One of the consistent lessons of a rising market is that the better the quality, the better the value as an asset for the future. Time and again, the man who has paid a very high price for a very fine painting or drawing has soon confounded those who shook their heads over the price at the time.

The difficulties involved in giving indications of prices are such that other writers have avoided the subject entirely. As I said in the introduction, I have chosen to cite gallery prices rather than saleroom prices, but in the following chapter, some reference will be made to saleroom prices.

Many of the problems are obvious. Variety within an artist's work may be so wide that corresponding price brackets are almost meaningless. As I have said, if a precedent is lacking in recent seasons, only an estimate of a painting's present value is possible. I have therefore been obliged to resort to estimation in the case of pictures sold say, three years ago, where no really comparable picture has since appeared on the market. If in doubt for one of these reasons, I have tried to err on the side of a higher rather than a lower figure.[1] Nothing is more daunting than to be told that an artist's work is available at such a figure, only to find, when you try to buy one, that the price is, in fact, higher and probably beyond your reach. If, of course, you find a good example below the price I have indicated,

[1] Hoping that my chapter will remain useful and realistic for the beginner for a few seasons.

so much the more encouraging. However, if you are offered one very far below the range, caution may be advisable. If people were as wary of being really under-charged as they are of being really over-charged, they would be well advised. In fact, if you are charged a very high price, provided the painting is a fine one, time may correct the situation, whereas if you pay a bargain price for something which turns out not to be genuine, time can hardly make it so.

Marines

Until recent years, English marine painting was denied the attention which it deserves, and I do not feel the situation has yet righted itself. How surprising in an essentially sea-going nation that marines could fall into neglect. Familiarity with the sea and ships may have led to indifference, perhaps the subject matter came to be thought too specialized, the province of its devotees alone. Whatever the reasons for disregard, I doubt if the pendulum has swung sufficiently the other way as yet, despite the present general revival of interest. If you are a lover of the sea, you will look with appreciation at the skill and understanding of marine painters in watercolours and oils, whereas, if you are a landlubber, the appeal and romance of marine painting must surely be felt. Although we are moving sadly away from the era of sea travel, more and more people are taking to sailing as a sport and, in a small way, recapturing the past. Whatever your personal attitude to the sea and its nostalgia, if you follow the artist's dictum that it is not what you paint but how you paint it that is important, then obviously marine painting ranks with any other contemporary subject matter. Often, in fact, it can be more challenging to the artist's powers than any other.

English marine painters of the eighteenth and nineteenth centuries were a highly professional body of men, whose work had often to pass the scrutiny of very knowledgeable and discerning patrons. In this respect, and in so many others, English marine painting followed the example of the great Dutch artists, Willem van de Velde the Elder (1611-93) and his son Willem (1633-1707) who lived in England from 1673 onwards. The most summary comparisons between eighteenth-century English painters and the Van de Veldes would show the latters' wide-reaching influence.[1] The work of the Van de Veldes is well represented, as are most English marine painters, at Greenwich. To journey down the Thames by launch and visit the National Maritime Museum is an ideal way of spending a summer day.[2]

In making my choice, I have avoided paintings which are of too specialized naval interest, for example, the ship 'portraits' which are more painted records than marine compositions, and the pure battle scenes which, however good as reminders of our all-important naval heritage, may be predominantly of historical rather than general artistic importance.

The Illustrations

Among the many painters who worked from first-hand knowledge of ships and the sea, was William Anderson (1757-1837).[3] A Scotsman brought up among shipwrights,

[1] Their drawings are of especial interest, and when using a specialist art library, take the opportunity of looking at the lavishly illustrated *Catalogue of the Van de Velde Drawings at the National Maritime Museum, Greenwich,* whose distinguished author, Michael Robinson, is the Museum's curator. This catalogue gives a wealth of fascinating technical explanation of the equipment and rigging of sailing ships.

[2] Details are in *Museums and Galleries* – boats leave from Westminster pier.

[3] Anderson is briefly discussed and illustrated by Hardie, *op. cit.,* and Colonel Grant, *The Old English Landscape Painters* (hereafter referred to as 'Grant').

Anderson came to London in his twenties, where he spent the remainder of his very long career, and established a fine reputation. His first painting to be exhibited at the Royal Academy (1787) was, 'A View on the Thames', and the life of the river remained his favourite subject. Although he was a regular contributor of oil paintings to the Royal Academy right into his seventies, the majority of his work was done in watercolour. A son, Guy, died from wounds at the Battle of Copenhagen.

Anderson is always acknowledged as one of the important marine painters, but he is an example of those artists whose work varies in quality very considerably. All his paintings are exact and minutely finished in those details of rigging and equipment which he knew so well. In his best work, he allied this detail and finish to an overall softness of colour, producing fine atmospheric effects, with clouds especially well put in.

Figure 3 shows a characteristic subject, the Thames at Rotherhithe, signed and dated 1790 on the spar in the foreground. Between the groups of ships, St Paul's is prominent in the background. This watercolour measures $8\frac{1}{4} \times 10\frac{1}{2}$ inches, typical of the small scale on which Anderson preferred to work.

In assessing any landscape or marine painting, topographical interest must be taken into consideration. In general, if there were two paintings or watercolours equally well done and in equally good condition, the one with an identifiable setting would be considered more valuable. Obviously, topography of London is especially choice, so that this drawing would have added importance and value for that reason. Apart from the subject matter however, as an example of Anderson's work, it has the qualities you would seek. Notice how expertly he has drawn the riggings of the two ships, lying stem to stern, with one partly seen across the other. In the same way, the figures are perfectly delineated both in the foreground and seated in the small craft. Foreground ripples and reflections on the water are particularly good, helping to lead the eye back into the distance, beneath the delicate washes of the sky.

Good watercolours by Anderson may range in price from £100 to £350.

An older contemporary of Anderson's, but destined to enjoy only half his lifespan, was John Cleveley Junior (1747-86).[1] Like Anderson, Cleveley was born into the world of ships, being the son of a shipwright or naval draughtsman at Deptford. Cleveley's good fortune was to be instructed in watercolour painting by Paul Sandby[2] during his period as drawing master at the Royal Military Academy, Woolwich. Although Cleveley painted in oils, watercolour remained his best medium. He too depicted scenes on the Thames, but his career took him far from his native surroundings. Twice in the 1770s he accompanied well recorded expeditions to the polar regions, and according to his exhibited works sailed as far as the Friendly Islands (Tonga). The travels of Cleveley and many others reflect the universal nature of British seapower throughout the period.

Figure 4 is a subject from Cleveley's voyaging, Belem Tower in the magnificent estuary of the Tagus at Lisbon.[3] The signature and date, 1778, are visible in the bottom left-hand corner – John's work should not be confused with that of his twin brother, Robert (1747-1809).

Again, with the realism of experience rather than imagination, Cleveley has depicted the choppy water, typical of an estuary in a strong wind. In the foreground, the crew of the

[1] See Hardie.

[2] See below.

[3] This watercolour is described and illustrated in colour in *Sea Painters of Britain* by F. G. Roe, plate 4 (published by Frank Lewis, 1947).

small craft are reefing in their sail, in what looks a hazardous operation. Their action, necessitated by the rising wind, is echoed by the diminishing line of boats away to the right. To the left, the sea breaks on rocks at the base of the famous tower. Even allowing for the difference in subject matter, Cleveley's handling seems more lively than that of Anderson's, but they share an ability to suggest spaciousness and depth, by the sky and the fall of light alone. Cleveley's colour in this example is more restrained than Anderson's and this is generally true. In assessing this drawing, remember that its important size, 18×24 inches, and topographical interest, would be factors. Cleveley's work is relatively rare, due in part to his early death. Examples of his watercolours range from £200 to £550.

A Bristol born artist, Nicholas Pocock (1741-1821)[1] might claim to head this group of seafaring painters, in terms of time at sea if not in terms of art. He did not give up his career as a mariner until the age of forty, although he had made sketches throughout his voyages. Encouraged by Sir Joshua Reynolds, Pocock eventually became a leading figure among the marine artists of his day. Figure 5 shows a typical example, signed and dated 1789, the year he settled in London. This foreign coastline is not identified. You will notice the 'dappled' brushwork, particularly noticeable in the darks of the foreground rocks, which is a little characteristic of Pocock's work. His colour scheme is light and soft, with blues, greens and pale yellows predominant, much warmer than the palette of Cleveley, for example. The launching of the boat is perfectly observed. Pocock painted landscapes as well as marines, and some of his watercolours were extremely accurately reproduced by

[1] See Randall Davies in Volume V of the *Old Watercolour Society's Annual Journal*, 1928. A full discussion of Pocock and a list of exhibited work. See also Hardie, *op. cit.*

coloured aquatint process. Thus, you must look closely at Pocock watercolours to avoid these aquatints, and this, of course, applies to other artists. It is fair to say that Pocock's extensive output is of uneven quality. Although small watercolours of landscapes are sometimes available for less than £100, landscapes of important size and good marines range from £120 to £450. In common with his contemporaries, Pocock made drawings of naval actions from which he painted large-scale oils of manoeuvres and battle scenes,[1] particularly from the Napoleonic War.

I have added, in contrast to the names of these famous marine painters, that of Henry Moses (*c*.1779-1860). This minor artist is known to me only from a pair of interesting oval drawings (Figs. 6 and 7).[2] They are a well contrasted pair, with a certain naïve charm, particularly in the slightly formalized treatment of the waves. They are examples of what may be found if you are on the lookout for worthy acquisitions by painters who are not necessarily familiar. Notice that the drawings have the artist's original washline mount in which he has put his signature and a precise date. There is also a monogram on one of the pair. Moses was active as an engraver of marine subjects too. I would expect his watercolours to range in price from £100 to £150.

Thomas Luny (1758-1837),[3] an almost exact contemporary of Anderson, was as well known as any marine painter of the period. Unlike the others, so far discussed, he did not paint in watercolour, but he shared their first-hand knowledge of the sea from service in the Napoleonic Wars. Luny was a West Countryman whose favourite subjects in later

[1] See Oliver Warner, 'Nicholas Pocock, Some Marine Watercolours of 1784', in the *Burlington Magazine*, November 1947, LXXXIX, pp. 317-18. This article discusses drawings in the British Museum.

[2] These drawings are illustrated in *A Dictionary of British Marine Painters*, by Arnold Wilson (Frank Lewis, 1967).

[3] See also Grant, *op. cit.*, and Arnold Wilson, *op. cit.*

years were of Teignmouth and the surrounding districts. In the last decade of his long career, the quality of his work sometimes deteriorated, but his best marine subjects are highly regarded. If in his later period, his palette became warmer, with stronger local colours, in his early work he followed the eighteenth-century tradition of restrained and subtle colouring. Figure 9 shows 'Shipping in Southampton Water', and is signed and dated 1788 in the left foreground. The sky is very freely painted in loose brush-strokes, to allow the light priming to provide luminosity. Luny's sea is a very realistic greeny-grey and the warm overall tone is typical of many of his pictures. Rigging and detail are, as we have seen throughout, competently handled. Do not underestimate the skill with which these highly professional marine painters make their ships and boats look as if they are really in the water and not simply placed on the surface.

Luny's work is extensive and he exhibited from his nineteenth year onwards. Examples of his later work are more readily available than those of his strictly eighteenth-century career. Good examples range from small canvases at £200 to his most important pictures at £1,500 or more.

One of the most distinguished names in marine painting is that of Serres. Dominic Serres (1722-93),[1] the father, belongs to the generation of Brooking, but his son, John Thomas Serres (1759-1825),[2] was a contemporary of Anderson and Luny. The younger Serres maintained the standard of his father's achievements in every way. Thus at the death of his father in 1793 he succeeded him as marine painter to the king on his own merits. He also came to hold the

[1] See below. Because of the rarity and therefore costliness of the elder Serres' marine work, I have preferred to discuss him in another context.

[2] The Serres family are yet to be explored in detail, but are well recorded in Grant and Hardie. A younger son, Dominic M. Serres, should not be confused with his father's signature.

position of draughtsman to the Admiralty. Unlike his fellow painters, so far discussed, security was denied to Serres. His very prosperous career was ruined by the scandalous activities of his wife, and his own disastrous speculation in theatrical investment. Tragically, J. T. Serres went to debtors prison and there he died.

However unkind the fates were to the man, Serres the artist gives no hint of it in his work. He was equally gifted in oils and watercolour, although the latter medium predominates. Serres drew with a vigorous strong line in a rapid, calligraphic manner which once you have seen, you would not mistake a second time. Many of his watercolours, both large and small, were painted in a long, panoramic format, and both his colours and lights and shadows tend to be more pronounced than an artist like Anderson or Cleveley.

Figure 8 is an example of his oil painting, 'Shipping off Leghorn',[1] which is signed and dated 1799, and inscribed 'Livorno'. The signature and inscription are easily seen on the wall in the foreground. Serres favoured the coast scene rather than the pure marine, and this has no doubt added to his admirers those who are not attracted by conventional marines. The sparkle and crispness of his technique as well as the choice of colour and the strong contrast of light and shadow, seem reminiscent of Canaletto. It is tempting to think Serres learnt from Canaletto's pupil, Samuel Scott (*c*.1702-72), a founder figure of the school. Certainly his way of painting architecture is reminiscent of William Marlow's (1740-1813), who was a pupil of Scott's for several years. The adjective calligraphic, used to describe his drawing style, is equally appropriate for his brushwork, in the treatment of the sea particularly. How rewarding either a book or an exhibition devoted to Serres would be.

[1] Illustrated in 'Round the Galleries' by Adrian Bury, *Connoisseur* (January 1967). Serres painted many pictures from his travels in France and Italy.

Good watercolours now range in price from £200 to £700, and oil paintings correspondingly higher.

Landscapes

Turning reluctantly from the sea and its coast, after a very selective discussion, I must now attempt the more difficult task of giving an idea of the achievement of English landscape painters. The predominance of landscape in one form or another as a subject matter is clear in oils and watercolours; its representation in this chapter reflects this position, and the wide choice available to the collector.

I have found it convenient, in arranging the artists, not to be bound too closely by either chronological order nor importance in terms of value; also watercolours are interspersed with oils.

The Eighteenth Century

A recent exhibition at Kenwood[1] drew some attention to an important artist, George Smith of Chichester (1714-76),[2] but he remains insufficiently appreciated. Such was not the case in his own lifetime, as he enjoyed a very considerable reputation and distinguished patronage. His name, like that of Joseph Wright of Derby, is always linked to his place of birth. Yet, unlike Wright and most other artists of the period, Smith remained in Sussex and achieved his fame even though he was away from London and other artistic centres, like Bath.

[1] 'The origins of English landscape'.

[2] Grant remains the main source of information about the Smith family. Unfortunately his entry on the artist is composed in his most rambling vein, but the appreciation of Smith's merits is to the late Colonel's great credit. At the time of writing, for general reading on the interpretation of landscape in painting, Sir Kenneth Clark's *Landscape into Art* has no equal (published in paperback by Penguin).

Smith's larger, more formal landscapes were based on the style of Claude Lorraine (1600-1682), whose classical landscapes of the Roman campagna were the ideal. Indeed, Claude's work was a major formulative influence on English taste in the eighteenth century. The landowners and farmers who were the majority of his patrons could not afford a Claude, even if they had wanted one, admired Smith for his own accomplishment and not only as a poor man's Claude. Otherwise, names like the Duke of Richmond[1] would not be among Smith's patrons.

Figure 10 is an example of Smith's larger, 'Claudian' manner, and a painting of considerable interest.[2] Smith contested and won the first premium (prize) for landscape painting with this painting in 1760. As with many of his compositions, the basis is a view down river towards Chichester, but any topographical fidelity is disguised by imaginary hills in the distance, and the Italianate buildings throughout the scene. On the right, in the foreground, there are portraits of George and his two brothers, William and John, who were also painters. George depicts himself standing with a scroll in hand, for he was also a poet of good merit, and perhaps thought of himself firstly as a poet rather than a painter. His palette is always restrained with many shades of browns, greens, and purple-greys. Very often, particularly in the distance, colours seem fused and misty in a most atmospheric way.

Figure 11 is by contrast an example of his small, rural landscapes which hold so much charm. From his treatment of foliage and his fine variations of darker hues, it is clear that he had studied not only Claude, but the great Dutch landscape painter, Jacob Ruisdael (1628-82). Yet, whatever

[1] Examples of Smith's larger pictures remain at Goodwood today.

[2] This painting was illustrated and discussed in 'Round the Galleries' *Connoisseur* (June 1965).

the influences from abroad, Smith is unmistakeably English in the mood of his Sussex landscapes. To quote Colonel Grant, 'None before him, and few since, have caught more perfectly than he the subtle aroma of the depths of our English countryside.' Two very characteristic details of Smith's work are the foreground foliage, clearly delineated compared to the 'blending' in the distance, and the profusion of birds in the sky. A note of particular interest in this Smith, is that it is the only signed example of the recorded collaboration of George and John. You will see that the signature in the bottom left foreground reads, 'G. & J. Smith'.

Figure 12 is an example of his much rarer Winter landscapes,[1] which are both romantic and decorative in a way that is easier seen than described. The ruined tower on the right and the cottage, are often included in his work, just as the highly individual way of treating the bare branches of the tree is peculiar to Smith. Again, the favourite *motif* of birds in flight is seen over a landscape which is more imagined than real.

In according George Smith of Chichester three illustrations, I have sought to emphasize the artistic competence and originality of his work as well as the variety and attractiveness of his compositions. The richness of his colouring cannot be shown here, but the tonal qualities are well illustrated in black and white.

No doubt Smith will eventually enjoy again the reputation he once had, and, on the evidence of his work, such a development would be entirely justified. Smith's paintings – he worked only in oils – are not of uniform attractiveness and quality, but good examples may range from £500 to £1,600. A celebrated pair of paintings,[2] which were en-

[1] See *Catalogue of the Mellon Collection, op. cit.*

[2] Entitled, 'The Hop Pickers', and 'The Apple Gatherers', these paintings are as much *genre* scenes as landscapes.

graved, are generally regarded as his finest works, and their exceptional status would, of course, be reflected in their value.

Smith's famous contemporary, Richard Wilson (1714-82),[1] would occupy a central position in any discussion of English landscape painting. His genuine work is rarely on the market and its value makes it irrelevant to the present context. I have therefore selected two of his pupils, whose work is accessible to the collector.

Thomas Jones (1742-1803) was, like Wilson, Welsh born. He became Wilson's pupil in 1763 and worked in Italy from 1776 to 1783. Figure 13 illustrates a signed example of his Wilsonesque landscapes; glowing with his master's warm light, and a reminder of Italy in the ruined, classical building. The way in which the sunlight is shown breaking through the foliage of the tree on the right, in small, bright streaks is also a purely Wilsonesque mannerism. Some idea of the difficulties of distinguishing the work of a painter from that of his pupil may be gathered from this entry in Jones' diary, confessing that he was 'guilty of a few innocent impostures by making imitations of my old master, Wilson . . . which passed among our connoisseurs at some of the publick sales for originals . . .' Yet Jones was a good painter in his own right. Perhaps you will detect his signature in the dark foreground of a landscape which has qualities but falls short of Wilson himself. Good examples may range from £450 to £1,200.

Joseph Farington (1747-1821) is celebrated for his massive diary, which was discovered in 1921, a new and most important source of information about different aspects of art and life in London from 1793-1821. Farington, like Jones, became a pupil of Wilson's in 1763, having come to London from his native Lancashire. A full account of his

[1] See W. G. Constable, *Richard Wilson.*

career as an Academician is given by Hardie. Farington's work in oils is virtually unknown today, but drawings certainly are available. The example illustrated, Figure 14, is a monochrome drawing, which is signed and dated 1792 in the foreground. Farington was notably a topographical draughtsman, many of whose drawings were engraved. As this drawing is of the Thames Valley, it may well have been in preparation for a publication by Farington in 1794, of seventy-six engraved views of the Thames. If you look closely at the illustration, you will see one or two pencilled colour notes.[1] In this case, the engravings were to be hand-coloured and these notes would have assisted in this work. Painters in oil and watercolour often made ink and wash drawings of this kind with colour notations, to remind them of the scene when they were back in their studios. Farington is especially well-represented in the V. & A. collection. His drawings may range from £150 to £500.

An earlier and more important name in topographical watercolours was the Swiss born artist Samuel Hieronymous Grimm (1733-94).[2] His early training of painting accurate Alpine views, determined his style of precise, fine drawing with pencil and pen, completed with very delicate watercolouring. In 1765, Grimm went to Paris where he stayed for three years before settling in England. His success was assured from the outset and he gathered an impressive list of patrons. Grimm drew figures extremely well and many of his works would properly be called *genre* scenes as much as landscapes. Figure 15 is a particularly fresh example, a view of Shire Green and Grenoside, Yorkshire, signed and dated 1781 in the right foreground. The minute pen strokes as in the wall and cottages, are a distinctive note of Grimm's

[1] In the sky and the nearest part of the river.

[2] See Hardie, and also Miss R. M. Clay, *S. H. Grimm* (Antiquary Books, 1941).

meticulous technique. In the same way, the tiny, curling lines of his foliage would be pointers to the authorship of an unsigned example. None the less, Paul Sandby often worked in watercolour in a manner very close to Grimm and, as Hardie points out, wrong attributions have been made between them. Grimm's important watercolours may range in price from £200 to £500. It is important to look at these exacting topographical views in the context of the later eighteenth century. The pleasures of travel and the appreciation of different scenery and architecture, both at home and on the Continent, were no longer the province of the aristocracy alone. The literature of the period, and particularly the poetry of Wordsworth and his contemporaries, were a major influence towards the love of nature, so apparent in the work of these artists for their patrons. The greatly increased publication of descriptive books, illustrated with engravings from their work, brought the appreciation of natural scenery and the talents of the artists to a wider public.

Artists like William Payne (1760-1830)[1] carried on, in the next generation, the tradition of precise topographical work. Payne began his career in Plymouth, and is said to have been self-taught and encouraged by his countryman, Sir Joshua Reynolds. He was a prolific and successful artist, and became a fashionable drawing master in London. Payne's favourite landscapes were those of the West Country and Figure 16 is a typical example, a distant view of Weymouth and Portland, which is signed but undated. In his watercolours, Payne favoured a dark, precise foreground, so giving greater depth to the misty blues and greens of the distance. His draughtsmanship is strong and fluent and

[1] See Basil S. Long, 'William Payne, Watercolour Painter Working 1776-1830', *Walker's Quarterly* (January 1922), which has a list of his many exhibited works.

41 FRANCESCO FERNANDI called IMPERIALI (1679–1741)
'The Contest of Apollo and Marsyas'
Oil on canvas
Size: 20¼ × 25¾ inches

42 HENRI-JOSEPH HARPIGNIES (1819–1916)
'A View of Lombardy'
Watercolour
Signed and dated 1861
Size: 9½ × 16½ inches

43 BERNARDUS-JOHANNES BLOMMERS (1845–1914)
'Beach Scene'
Oil on canvas laid down on board
Signed
Size: 4¾ × 7¼ inches

44 JEAN-LÉON GÉRÔME (1824–1904)
'A View of Jerusalem'
Oil on canvas,
Signed and inscribed
Size: $8\frac{3}{4} \times 12$ *inches*

45 JEAN-LÉON GÉRÔME
'A View of Baalbek'
Oil on canvas,
Signed and inscribed
Size: $8\frac{3}{4} \times 12$ *inches*

46 MAURICE COURANT (1847–1925)
'Beach Scene'
Oil on canvas
Signed and dated 1906
Size: $18\frac{3}{8} \times 15$ inches

although his treatment of foliage is reminiscent of Grimm, it is looser and more rapidly described. Payne's watercolours may range from less than £100 to £300.

Moses Griffith (1749-*c.*1810),[1] was definitely a self-taught artist whose talents would not have emerged but for his being taken up by his patron, the naturalist Thomas Pennant. Griffith, born in Caernarvonshire, was of very humble origin and in his diary Pennant speaks of him as of a well-liked and very useful servant whom he kept with him on his travels to make drawings from which the naturalist's books were illustrated. Figure 17 is identified as Llanbedr Hall, Denbighshire, from the artist's inscription on the back. His signature and the date, 1 August 1805, are also on the reverse. Although Griffith's drawing style and his choice of colour are like those of Grimm, he is by no means in the same category of importance. A comparison of the illustrations underlines this point.

Griffith's work only became known in any quantity when two thousand drawings by him were discovered and sold in 1938; there was an exhibition of his drawings at the Walker Gallery in 1939.

Until recent years, a good collection of watercolours might have been formed with many examples purchased for under £100. However discouraging it may be to those with very limited budgets, the fact is that only by careful selection can a really worthwhile watercolour now be bought for less than this amount. By worthwhile, I mean of course authentic, representative of the artist, attractive in itself, and in good condition. I mention 'representative of the artist' because some of the very small, fragmentary drawings are so slight that, even if unquestionably genuine, they cannot

[1] See Hardie, and Iolo Williams, 'Thomas Pennant and Moses Griffith, a Welsh Naturalist and his Welsh Artist in the Eighteenth Century', *Country Life* (July 1938).

really stand as the representation of that particular artist in a collection.

Opportunities for buying for less than £100 occur in the case of minor artists whose names are not well known. For example, Figure 18 is a watercolour by the French born Peter La Cave (active 1769-1810), a minor figure who is not, for example, mentioned in books like Hardie. None the less, his work has charm and he is represented in the V. & A. collection by several comparable drawings. This little example, 7×10 inches is signed and dated 1801,[1] in the bottom left corner, and the presence of La Cave's signature is particularly relevant. He is an artist whose name is loosely applied to drawings which otherwise would be difficult to attribute. In style, he is slightly reminiscent of Julius Caesar Ibbetson[2] and his work has probably passed under that distinguished name. Although La Cave worked principally in England, he retained a slight Continental note in his drawing and choice of colour. In this rural scene, pale blues and blue-greens and greys predominate. Incidentally, there is a good example of a 'drag' stroke in the foreground. The slight surface texture of the paper is the equivalent of the canvas weave in oil paintings, and colour only 'catches' on the tops and leaves the paper showing in the hollows as the fairly dry brush is 'dragged' across. Doubtless, research would reveal more information about La Cave and others like him, but they must wait their turn until much more important artists have received the scholarly attention due to them. Larger examples of La Cave's work might well be outside the price range of this particular example.

Reverting to the well-known topographers of the eighteenth and early nineteenth centuries, Francis Nicholson (1753-1844) is an artist whose life began in the reign of

[1] La Cave exhibited at the Royal Academy in this year.

[2] See below.

George II and ended in the seventh year of Queen Victoria's. Into this long career Nicholson put untiring effort, and from simple beginnings in his native Yorkshire became not only a successful artist but a writer on the technique of watercolour,[1] a founder of the Old Water Colour Society in London, and later its President.

Nicholson's work is not uniform, particularly in his later years, but at his best he deserves perhaps more recognition than at present. I have accorded him two examples because he receives little mention in Hardie, surprisingly, and no illustrations. After Yorkshire, Nicholson's favourite subject was Scotland, which he toured under the patronage of the Earl of Bute.

Figure 19 is a particularly pleasing example, a view of Loch Lomond, signed and dated 1794 on the artist's mount, and inscribed on the reverse. His colouring is usually soft and delicate with very good tonal values. The attractiveness of his work is augmented by the well placed and very well drawn figures. Although there is no direct connection, of course, he strikes one as a landscape counterpart to William Anderson. Figure 20 shows Nicholson's abilities at architectural, urban subjects; it is of 'The Grass Market',[2] signed and dated 1807, and carefully inscribed by the painter, 'From the corner of the Grass Market, Edinburgh'. This watercolour has the characteristic 'glow' which is often to be found with Nicholson. His palette is often rich in browns and tawny colours, as in this example for the stonework of the Scottish capital. Nicholson's work may range in price from £120 to £500.

[1] An interesting illustration of the build-up of a watercolour from Nicholson's book is reproduced in the book already discussed, W. G. Constable, *The Painter's Workshop.*

[2] This watercolour was exhibited at the Old Water Colour Society in 1807, No. 313.

As I have said when discussing J. T. Serres, his father's – Dominic Serres (1722-93) – marine work, particularly his watercolours, is rare, so much so that it seemed impractical to include him under that heading. However, by exploring the lesser known aspects of an artist's output, you may acquire a good example of his work at an advantageous price. Serres, father and son, are recorded as having painted landscapes, and Grant includes a mention of these in their entry. Dominic Serres, who was born at Auch in Gascony, ran away to sea and rose from common seaman to the command of a merchantman. He was captured by the English in the 1750s and taken a prisoner to England. He was released on parole and soon became a very good marine painter. Through the help of Charles Brooking, Serres flourished and gained his royal appointment and the position of Librarian to the Royal Academy, where he was a regular exhibitor.

Figure 21 is an example of his landscape work from his early years in England, being signed and dated 1762. His use of delicate blue-greens and russet colours, particularly in the foliage, are distinctive and reminiscent of his French origin. The brushwork is clear and sharp in highlights, like the dog which drinks from the stream, and softer in a Smith of Chichester manner among the foreground and trees. You can see the characteristic eighteenth-century *craquelure* in this photograph. Landscapes by Dominic Serres may range in price from £450 to £800. Admittedly they are rare, but I have chosen him as an example of investigating the scope of an artist's work to your advantage.

By the same token, bearing in mind that Richard Wilson earned his living at the start of his career by portraiture, you may discover one – unlikely perhaps, but less so than with a landscape!

Because the landscapes of Richard Wilson and Gainsborough are, for practical purposes, no longer available, attention has focused on those painters who used to be called minor masters. The results are twofold. Firstly, the obvious one that they have risen in value, and secondly, that apart from other considerations, their own merits are better appreciated.

Such has been the case with two very fine landscape painters, Julius Caesar Ibbetson (1759-1817) and Paul Sandby (1725-1809). Their status has yet to be properly established in relation to other painters, particularly so Ibbetson. Ibbetson was the subject of a book by Miss Rotha Mary Clay, published in 1948. Because this book is rich in biographical detail, there is a fascinating opportunity to follow the eventful life of the painter. However, only a relatively small number of his pictures are illustrated, and many important pictures were unknown to the writer. I say this without reproach, because any art historical book benefits from revision after twenty years.

Ibbetson, who began as a ship painter in Hull, then a theatrical scene painter, first worked in London copying Dutch seventeenth-century paintings, an occupation which decisively influenced his own style. In 1788, he was appointed draughtsman to an expedition to China which took him as far as Java, before the death of the leader meant Ibbetson's return to England. Do not, therefore, turn away from a drawing of natives or a watercolour of a flying fish as things which could not be from the hand of an English landscape painter! His wife's death in 1794 was followed by domestic and financial troubles until he moved from London. He lived first near Ambleside and went to Scotland in 1800, before finally settling at Masham, in his native Yorkshire.

Both the style and the quality of his work varies, and is confused by the inclusion of many pictures which are, in fact, by Rathbone, La Cave, and others. However, his genuine work always has quality, the majority of his paintings and drawings were of rural life, with farms and animals, in the same vein as his friends George Morland (1763-1804) and James Ward (1769-1859). When Ibbetson turned away from the countryside to depict elegant figures in landscapes, principally during his years in London, he produced his most desirable work in both oil and watercolours equally well.

Figures 22 and 23 illustrate a notable pair of drawings, with promenading figures at Kilburn, and in the background a distant view of London, with St Paul's clearly visible. Each is signed and dated 1787, and inscribed 'Kilburn', where the artist actually lived at this period. The superb figure groups and the fresh, delicate colours, could not I feel be bettered by Wheatley or any other painter of the age. The dark patches of moss and foliage in the foreground, put in with sooty-black are a little mannerism of Ibbetson's work.

In a most interesting way, Ibbetson used both the figure groups in these two drawings in an important painting of the same year, as seen in Figure 24. Ibbetson exhibited this painting, which is entitled 'A View of Harrow from Kilburn',[1] at the Royal Academy in 1787 (No. 142), and it has been twice exhibited in more recent times. In this sort of painting, Ibbetson uses the most subtle colours and paints with very delicate glazes. In terms of quality, subject, and topographical importance, this example may fairly be said to represent Ibbetson at his best. Clearly, paintings of this kind are rarely on the market, but in all good Ibbetsons there is much to be recommended. Examples of his work vary correspondingly in price. A first-class watercolour will

[1] The spire of Harrow Church is clearly seen on the top of the Hill on the skyline.

bring as much as, and occasionally more than, a good painting. Despite Ibbetson's importance and the recent interest in him, his good paintings and drawings still range in price from £800 to £3,500.

Paul Sandby[1] has come to be recognized as a central figure in the development of the English watercolour school.

In the tradition of the topographers, he was technically a superb craftsman who industriously studied his methods and mediums to reach perfection.[2] Yet, if he was the culmination of the topographical movement, he was also something outside it, Sandby brought to realism the eye of a true artist, at once poetic and romantic. By all accounts, he was a charming, accomplished and friendly man, and one senses this, perhaps, from his simple watercolours of rural life. Figure 25 shows a woman gathering fuel with her child in Windsor Great Park. The castle is just visible in the distance.[3]

Perhaps you may best see for yourself why I have described Sandby's work as poetic realism. His lightness and freshness of colour add a further note of enchantment to his compositional style. He worked as happily in oils, although these are rare compared to watercolours and gouaches. Figure 27 is an oil painting of Pembroke Castle from the West, which Sandby exhibited at the Royal Academy in 1808 (No. 565). This picture is painted on paper stuck down on panel, with the rich brown colour of the paper acting as a priming. Sandby uses this underlying

[1] See William Sandby, *Thomas and Paul Sandby* (London 1892); *Catalogue of the Sandby Exhibition at the Guildhall* (1960); and Grant, Hardie.

[2] Sandby was a very fine figure painter, an etcher, and was responsible for the first use of aquatint engraving in England.

[3] The finest collection of Sandby's drawings is at Windsor. See Paul Oppé, *The Drawings of Paul Sandby and Thomas Sandby at Windsor Castle* (1947).

colour particularly in the trees, working with many fine glazes. Indeed, the beauty of the painting derives from this fine, rich 'transparency'. The highlights are sharp accents which give the final sparkle, especially on the shimmering surface of the water.

What are regarded as Sandby's most important paintings are those done in gouache. This French term is used to describe opaque watercolour, which is made by adding Chinese white to the watercolour pigments. The gouache medium was principally used on the Continent in preference to pure watercolour, and it requires considerable practice in use because the colour when wet is so much darker than when it dries. The painter in gouache must allow for this in deciding his tonal values. Gouache is also called body-colour, and you must distinguish between a work done purely in gouache and a conventional watercolour which has been 'heightened' with touches of opaque colour.

In using gouache, Sandby primed the paper first because, unlike transparent watercolour, it is not to sink into the surface. As with oils, the artist working in gouache can work up to the lights, whereas in pure watercolour, of course, the artist works away from the light paper to the darks. A full understanding of Sandby's wonderful mastery of this medium, and the quality of his painting at its best, did not really come about until 1965. An important group of gouache paintings from the collection of the Earl of Harewood was sold at Christie's for prices ranging from 5,000 to 8,500 guineas within a group of five paintings. These drawings were of exceptional topographical value, four views of Windsor[1] and a military encampment in St James's Park.

Figure 26 is an example of Sandby's gouache painting,

[1] Sandby worked frequently at Windsor where his brother Thomas held the post of Deputy Ranger of Windsor Forest.

a view of Cory-lin on the Upper Clyde,[1] which is signed in the left foreground. Obviously this example is not comparable in importance to the famous ones I have just mentioned, but then neither was it sold for the same price – nor anything like! It is still possible to buy good examples of this kind, and I have illustrated it not only for that reason, but because it shows another facet of his style. Sandby could introduce a strongly romantic note into appropriate scenery, faintly recalling the mood of Salvator Rosa whose works were then so popular in England. The way he has handled the clouds, for example, heightens the dramatic effect of the rugged landscape with strongly silhouetted ruins. Yet it was the naturalism of Sandby in such work as the watercolour illustrated which most impressed his contemporaries. Gainsborough referred to him as 'the only man of genius' who had painted 'real views from Nature in this country'. Because of Sandby's versatility in three mediums, it falls within the means of collectors to acquire perhaps some example of his work. Good watercolours may range in price from £300 to £850; oil paintings are very difficult to assess, but roughly £700 to £1,200 and gouaches from £1,500 to £5,000.

The new collector should not be deterred from trying to acquire an example of an important artist, like Sandby or better still an Ibbetson, even though their finest works may be well outside his price range. The values can be deceptive. In any case, even if you spent a few thousand in buying the very finest, the value of these artists' work is still only a small fraction of a landscape by a lesser artist of the Impressionist period. In my view, Sandby and Ibbetson represent the best available landscape painters of the eighteenth century, allowing that Scott, Marlow, and Wright of Derby are,

[1] Sandby was employed as a young man in survey work in Scotland and painted many views of the inspiring scenery.

like Richard Wilson, now beyond the ordinary collector's reach.

In the same way, I would cite three other watercolours which are modest but very worthy examples of major artists. Figure 28, entitled 'Travellers on Bodmin Moor', is a good representation of the work of one of the best-known of all English watercolourists, Thomas Rowlandson (1756-1827).[1] The strong, dark line of his looping pen work gives the vitality to his work. To what extent Rowlandson was influenced in this style of drawing by his stay in Paris in 1771-2, is an interesting point. Many of Rowlandson's best drawings are unsigned and signatures have been added in the nineteenth century to drawings which were not by him. You must look for the characteristically jaunty drawing style as a signature, especially the way he draws horses, which feature in most of his landscapes. Drawings of this kind may range in price from £300 to £700, whereas caricature and narrative drawings may be twice this last figure, and in certain instances more.[2]

John Constable, RA (1776-1837) was a tireless draughtsman who, in common with so many landscape painters, was never without his sketching notebook. Individual sheets from these many books show the essence of his style, and you can sense the greatness in the least of his hurried jottings. From a notebook of 1832-3, of which other leaves are known, comes this pencil and watercolour sketch, Figure 31, which is inscribed in his handwriting with the location, Buckden, Yorkshire, and the date, 1832. The remarkable feature of such drawings by the great masters, is the sense of volume or roundness in a three-dimensional

[1] A. P. Oppé, *Thomas Rowlandson, His Drawings and Watercolours* (1923); F. Gordon Roe, *Rowlandson, The Life and Art of a British Genius* (F. Lewis, 1947).

[2] See next Chapter.

way, which apparently haphazard touches of the pencil or crayon can build up. Examples of this kind range in price from £400 to £800, whereas oil sketches must bring thousands rather than hundreds, and more important examples can be discounted on grounds of rarity on the market.

A younger contemporary of Constable's, John Sell Cotman (1782-1842) is the greatest exponent of watercolour in the distinguished Norwich school. Cotman's watercolours of his mature period are now valued in thousands, but occasionally his early works are available at much more amenable figures. Figure 30 of Leatherhead church is signed and dated 1800, which the eighteen-year-old artist sent to the Royal Academy in that year (No. 424). The colouring of this early watercolour is in the restrained, almost monochrome palette typical of Girtin and the early Turner. Cotman met these artists at this period when they gathered at the home of Dr Munro. The value of modern, specialist books for the collector is neatly summarized by two quotations from an excellent book, *Watercolours of the Norwich School*, by Derek Clifford (Cory, Adams & MacKay, 1965). Cotman was the head of a family of artists and his children helped him when he was drawing master at Kings College, London. It was a hectic period and Cotman wrote of it: 'Edmund, Ann, Alfred and I are all drawing mad; Ann and Alfred working for the college pupils, with great effect in every way. They have done crack subjects, and they take wonderfully. Little do they (the students) ken by whom the drawings are done when given under my name.' Forewarned by such information, the informed collector would avoid doubtful examples of Cotman's work at this period.

To another provincial centre, Liverpool, belongs a very different contemporary of Cotman's, Charles Towne (1763-1840). Towne was an animal painter who was influenced by Stubbs, and also by Dutch masters like Cuyp. His name has come to prominence only in recent years, due in part to the rise of sporting paintings. Although Towne painted fine hunting and racing subjects, as well as animal portraits, his scenes of horses and cattle at rest in a landscape, may be of more general interest. Figure 29 is an important example whose rich, glowing colour and crisp highlights are particularly reminiscent of the same type of scene by the great Dordrecht painter of the seventeenth century, Aelbert Cuyp (1620-91). Towne's paintings are often signed, as is the case here, with a small 'CT' monogram. The prices of his work range from less than £1,000 up to £5,000 for his major sporting pictures whose subject matter, as I have said, is very important today in assessing market values.

Portraiture

The heyday of buying English portraiture belonged to the Duveen[1] era, when the enthusiasm of American millionaires pushed the values of eighteenth-century portraits to undreamed of levels. Although portraits have by no means recaptured those values, there has been a marked revival of interest both in the major and minor artists over the last decade. Among the minor figures, were portrait painters of great charm, yet their work is still comparable in price with some of the watercolour landscapes.

John Downman (1750-1824) was a successful portraitist, who preferred to work in watercolour, producing highly finished, lightly coloured likenesses of his sitters. He seems to have been an industrious artist in demand with all the great families of the day, and painting members of the Royal Houses of both England and Prussia. Because of this

[1] The career of Joseph Duveen, the most remarkable of art dealers, is very amusingly related in *Duveen* by J. N. Behrman (Hamish Hamilton, 1952).

preferred watercolour technique, Downman was not regarded as a major figure by his contemporaries, and he quarrelled with the Royal Academy for treating his portraits as drawings and thus relegating them to a lesser room in the exhibition of 1784. The portrait of Mary Seawell of Great Bookham, Figure 34, is typical of Downham's graceful interpretation of the sitter, worked with very delicate pencil strokes and lightly coloured with pinks and blues. It is signed and dated 1792. Portraits of this kind may range in price from less than £100 to £300.

In contrast to the Downman, the portrait of a young girl, Figure 32, by John Russell (1744-1806)[1] is richly coloured with the young girl dressed in a scarlet cloak and a black bonnet, set against a steely-blue ground. The difference in colour is partly due to the use of pastel rather than watercolour. Pastel is a medium consisting of pure pigment and pipeclay bound together with a small amount of gum. The pastels are very fragile sticks that give the softest powdery effect on the surface of the paper. Pastel is difficult to use and to preserve, for the slightest touch will disturb the surface. John Russell even used to stick a little handbill on to the back of his pictures giving advice on the care of pastels. He also wrote *Elements of Painting with Crayons* (1772). Pastels were popular with the French portraitists like Perroneau (1715-83) whose charming 'Girl with a Kitten' at the National Gallery is a masterpiece of the technique.

John Russell studied the great Continental pastellists and also the work of Reynolds whom he greatly admired, and was in his day very highly honoured with titles such as 'Painter to the King and Prince of Wales'. Today this high reputation is understandably questionable, although his pastels of children have an undeniable charm and tender-

[1] See J. I. Smith, 'The Tempestuous Life of John Russell, RA', *Connoisseur* (October 1965).

ness. Russell pastels may vary in price from £200 to £600 depending, as with all portraits, on the attractiveness of the sitter.

Captain Edward Becher, Figure 33, painted by Sir Martin Archer Shee (1769-1850) is celebrated as the first man over the Brook on the Aintree racecourse, now known as Becher's Brook. The fact that the sitter of this portrait is both identified and a figure of some historical interest, must be taken into consideration in pricing a picture such as this, yet it is often possible to get fine, unidentified portraits by the lesser masters of the eighteenth century for little over £100 – portraits that are both worthwhile and highly decorative.

The Nineteenth Century

Clearly, my purpose has been to concentrate on English painting in the eighteenth and early nineteenth centuries. In order to do so, I was obliged to choose a more summary means of discussing other fields.

Landscape and marine painting lost nothing of their status in the Victorian age. The sentiment, interpretation, and colouring changed in a manner that is immediately discernible, and is shared by the other arts. The industry and technical competence of the artists did not change. However, the spread of wealth meant an ever-widening market, to which some of the lesser artists responded with very mechanical, uninspired productions. There is sometimes an absence of that sincerity so apparent in the financially less successful painters of the previous age.

James Holland (1800-1870)[1] is certainly one of the best known painters of the period. His first job as a ceramic

[1] See Randall Davies, 'James Holland', in the Old Water Colour Society's *Journal* (1930).

flower painter probably, as with Renoir, developed his sense of light, fresh colour. Although he painted endlessly in England, he is most esteemed for his Venetian scenes. Holland in his day has been dubbed second only to Turner in capturing the colour and atmosphere of the 'Queen of the Adriatic'. He travelled extensively too in the rest of Europe, never allowing his exuberance to carry him away from topographical accuracy. Holland naturally developed tremendous facility in drawing and painting, both in oil and watercolour. The large-scale, more formal oils may tend to hide his gifts as a draughtsman.

Figure 36 is an excellent example of the vitality he can put into a small watercolour. This page from a sketchbook, smaller than that of Constable, shows Guardi-like figures making their way in a breeze on the foreshore of Margate. The watercolour is inscribed and dated 23 September 1861. Small watercolours of this kind may range from £100 to £300, compared to the much higher prices for oils.

The seaside resort was a largely English innovation, which was becoming universally popular at this period. Figure 35 is a view of neighbouring Broadstairs by George Chambers (1803-40). Chambers, born at Whitby, left a seafaring apprenticeship and came to London. His promising career as a marine painter was cut short by his early death at the age of thirty-seven. Chambers painted Broadstairs in the manner of an oil sketch, compared to his stiffer brushwork in larger works. The new-fangled bathing machines are a particularly charming detail. Bleak House, of Dickens fame, is seen on the headland, in its original architectural form. Small oil paintings of this kind may range in price from £250 to £650.

James Baker Pyne (1800-1870) was an exact contemporary of Holland, although not his equal in painting. Pyne was a Bristol born painter, the teacher of Müller, who may aptly be called a Turneresque artist. He travelled in Italy and produced many very pleasing and romantic views of Venice and the Italian lakes. The colours are light and glowing, and Pyne's technique always seems that of a watercolourist working in oils, although he was equally at home in either medium. Figure 37, a view of Lake Maggiore with the Post-town of Luino, is representative of Pyne in this vein. For the major part of his career, Pyne kept a handwritten record of his paintings, corresponding to the numbers after the signature, for example in this case, the painting is signed and dated 1869 and numbered 726. Pyne's *Picture Memoranda* is preserved in the V. & A. Library. Pyne was a very prolific artist whose work extends from small watercolours under £100 to oils up to ten times that amount, although this figure would be reserved for a painting of exceptional importance.

Among these artists, the Scotsman David Roberts (1796-1864)[1] was the most renowned in his lifetime. His career provides a success story in the best tradition. From simple beginnings in Edinburgh, Roberts worked his way, through years of house decorating and scene painting, to recognition and fame. The honours accorded to him were civic as well as artistic, for six years before his death, he received the freedom of his native city. Roberts' reputation was founded on his architectural scenes from every corner of Europe and the Middle East, a prodigiously energetic painter, whose output in both oils and watercolour rivalled that of his friend Turner.

In preference to a stirring and romantic scene from his many travels, I have chosen a Scottish subject, the Priory of Pluscardine, Morayshire, as an example of Roberts in his

[1] See J. Ballantine, *The Life of David Roberts, RA* (Edinburgh, 1866); T. Quigley, 'David Roberts RA as a Watercolour Painter', *Walker's Quarterly* (January 1923).

47 PIETER WITHOOS (1654–93)
'A Garden Tulip'
Gouache
Signed and dated 1683
Size: $12\frac{5}{8} \times 8$ *inches*

48 PIETER WITHOOS
'A Garden Tulip'
Gouache
Signed and dated 1683
Size: $12\frac{5}{8} \times 8$ inches

most sincere and truly artistic manner. This watercolour, Figure 40, is inscribed and dated on the left in pencil, and signed on the right. The colouring is restrained in the eighteenth-century manner with greens predominant, and is an excellent demonstration of using bodycolour sparingly and effectively to heighten a pure watercolour, notably in the architecture and the foreground rocks on the right. Watercolours of this kind may range in price from £120 to £250, but the prices of Roberts' work vary with the subject matter, size, medium, in the usual way. Oils and watercolours of architectural subjects may cost from £500 to £1,300, and exceptional paintings such as full-scale Venetian views several thousand pounds.

Another painter, born in the same year as Holland and Pyne was James Wilson Carmichael (1800-1868).[1] In the nineteenth century, Carmichael represents the continuing tradition of marine painters who were brought up with the ways of ships and the sea. He was also a landscape painter, and the majority of his marines are coastal views. Carmichael has no biographer as yet, nor are there more than a few brief notices in periodicals, but his name is now deservedly becoming well known. Certainly, he was much before the public eye in his career, both in the North of England – he was born at Newcastle – and in London. In common with all these artists, Carmichael worked for publishers, and his most notable volume was *English Coast Views from the Mouth of the Thames to the Firth of Forth.* Carmichael was also employed by the *Illustrated London News* as a war artist in the Crimea in 1855-6, who published many of his sketches. At his best, he is an excellent marine painter, whose colour and tonal qualities are often better than many of his contemporaries. I have illustrated examples of his marine and landscape work.

[1] See Grant.

The calm sea with its well observed reflections gives especial merit to Figure 38, a scene of 'Shipping off Portsmouth', which is signed and dated 1863. Carmichael's 'View of Durham', Figure 39, is painted in a freer style, reminiscent of the 'View of Broadstairs' by Chambers. By coincidence, both paintings are on artists' millboard, which was specially manufactured by firms like Winsor and Newton, and widely used. The great Cathedral, the river with its bridge, make a splendid composition. Carmichael is particularly adept at putting in figures on a very small scale with tiny touches of sharp colour and impasto. In the original, for example, which measures 9×13 inches, the figures crossing the bridge are typical.

Carmichael's good marines and landscapes range in price from £300 to £1,200, including the rare and very desirable topographical views in London. Watercolours may be less than £100, and there is a particularly good example in the V. & A.

Some Suggestions from Other Schools

Amid the clamour surrounding the names of the great Impressionists, there is a tendency to ignore many interesting painters who were their contemporaries. Of such artists, Henri-Joseph Harpignies (1819-1916) is well known. Although he did not take to painting seriously until he was over thirty, as it was to turn out, he had the length of a normal career still before him, living to the age of ninety-seven. Harpignies was a superb watercolour painter who was particularly influenced by Corot in his early work. In short, he became celebrated in the academies of France and a distinguished exhibitor at the Water Colour Society in London. Oil paintings by Harpignies are still available, but his watercolours are more appropriate in price for the beginner. I have illustrated a fine and relatively costly example, Figure 42, 'A View in Lombardy', signed and dated 1861. It is one of those watercolours whose freshness and pristine condition belie their age. The predominant colours here are the dark greens and blues, with pale greys in the distant mountains. Watercolours by Harpignies may range in price from £150 to £700. There has not been an important exhibition of his work for a decade, and I am sure it would be a rewarding experience.

Those who admire, as I do, the wonderful Italian views by Corot, will find another echo of their influence in the work of Jean-Léon Gérôme (1824-1904).[1] Gérôme did not confine himself to landscape painting, nor indeed to painting itself, for he turned to sculpture in his later years. Many of his paintings are very academic, particularly the historical and religious subjects. However, he travelled widely like David Roberts, and painted realistic landscapes from his journeys. I have illustrated such a pair of Jerusalem and Baalbek, which are signed, inscribed with the location in each case, Figures 44 and 45. They succeed in conveying the desert atmosphere, and the buildings seem to shimmer in the heat. Landscapes of this kind by Gérôme range in price from £200 to £400.

A lesser known artist of the same period was Maurice Courant (1847-1925) who painted charming coastal scenes in an Impressionist palette and style. I have illustrated an example, Figure 46, signed and dated 1906, of a moonlit beach, where the softness of the light is well suggested by the transparent and fluid brushstrokes. There are many small masters of the French nineteenth-century school who, like

[1] See Moreau-Vauthier, *Gérôme Peintre et Sculpteur* (Paris, Hachette, 1906). There has recently been a Gérôme exhibition at the Vasser College Art Gallery, which was reviewed in the *Burlington Magazine* (June 1967, page 375).

Courant, may reward investigation, and I have drawn attention to him as much for this reason as for his own merits. His paintings may range from £150 to £300.

Beach scenes by Eugène Boudin (1824-98)[1] and the Dutch-born Jongkind (1819-91) have become extremely popular and must now be valued in thousands. As with the French school, there were minor artists who have been overshadowed by the great names but may now, when these are no longer available, receive greater attention. For example, Bernardus-Johannes Blommers (1845-1914)[2] was a distinguished figure in his day. He was encouraged by other painters in The Hague school, notably Maris and Israels. Blommers specialized in painting simple scenes from the beach whose monetary values in proportion to artists like Jongkind and Boudin are not a fair reflection on their relative artistic merits. I have illustrated a typical small oil by Blommers, Figure 43, which is signed to the bottom right. His work ranges in price from less than £100 to £700, particularly in Holland.

It may be of interest to compare values, by illustrating two paintings of an entirely different kind. Figure 41 is a painting by an Italian artist of the early eighteenth century, Francesco Fernandi (1679-1741)[3] who is usually called Imperiali after the name of his patron, Cardinal Imperiali. His work was especially popular with English patrons on the Grand Tour, hence the presence of his pictures in many country houses. Imperiali also worked in Spain and made a considerable reputation with his religious and mythological

[1] See *The Times*, Sotheby Index (25 November 1967).

[2] See *Dutch Painting in the Nineteenth Century*, by J. Hermine Marius (London 1908), page 34; and Max Rooses, *Dutch Painters of the Nineteenth Century* (London 1898).

[3] See Professor Waterhouse, 'Arte Lombarda' (1958, No. 3). This article discusses his English pupils and his work in English private collections. See also M. Clark, 'Imperiali', *Burlington Magazine* (May 1964), page 226.

subjects. Illustrated here is 'The Musical Contest of Apollo and Marsyas', a characteristic mythology. Marsyas found the pipes of Pan and challenged Apollo to a musical contest in which, as can be seen in the painting, King Midas has unfairly decided that Marsyas is the victor. Apollo, angered at this injustice, has turned the ears of Midas, Marsyas and his follower, into asses' ears. The poses of the figures are typical of the classical training of an Italian artist. The palette is very rich, with the dark greens and browns of the foreground giving way to the deep blues of the hills in the distance. Examples of this kind may range in price from £700 to £2,000.

Still-life and flower painting have leapt to the forefront of popularity in the last few years. Whether it is admiration for the perfection of technique displayed in these pictures particularly of the Dutch and Flemish seventeenth century, or whether it is the attraction of a timeless and to some extent abstract subject matter, is debatable. More probably it is the simple beauty of these paintings which has brought them into line with the values of Dutch painting in other subjects. The consequent rise in value has tended to place good flower paintings of the seventeenth century in a price range of thousands rather than hundreds of pounds. None the less, if you are attracted by early flower paintings, there are occasionally opportunities to buy the watercolour and gouache studies from which the flower painters composed their bouquets. In this way, they were able to paint a composition with flowers of different seasons, and they had a permanent record of rare and unrepeatable blooms. These parchment sheets were often handed down within the family or studio of an artist, so that certain flowers are recognized from one generation to the next. Figures 47 and 48 illustrate examples of these gouache studies by Pieter Withoos (1654-93), the son of Mathias Withoos, who like his father was a fine flower painter. The artist's signature and date (1683) are in the bottom right-hand corner. Like the English watercolours, with proper framing and mounting these flower studies might take the place of a painting in oils. The preservation of these gouaches in perfect condition is yet another example of the permanence of paintings when they are given reasonable care. Examples of this kind range in price from £150 to £300.

Perhaps you have found some of these suggestions accord with your own tastes and that they may form a point of departure for your collection, as they have for many of their present owners.

5 Investment and the Care of Paintings

This Chapter is short. If you read newspapers, listen to the radio, watch television or talk to people, you will be aware that paintings have gone up in value. If you do all of these, as most of us do, you will be more than well aware of it. As inflation weakens the value of money, the price of such things as land and old paintings of which there is an immutable quantity, goes up. Neither has any intrinsic worth but derives its value from what we are prepared to pay for it. You might argue that land is a necessity and paintings are not, but your mistake in doing so would be to demote our existence to a mundane level.

Nature has only given some of us creative gifts, but the power of appreciation she gives to all.

In many respects, the new collector would have an advantage in knowing nothing of the change in values. He would be free of preconceived ideas which tend to make the more experienced retrospective in their thinking. The further back one goes, to immediate post-war times, to pre-war days, to before the First World War and beyond, the more striking contrasts and contradictions are to be found. Of the legion numbers of examples, we will confine ourselves to one in each category.

In 1945 a gentleman bought a watercolour in an antique shop near Bishops Stortford for one pound. It turned out to be a large and very famous Rowlandson of Vauxhall Gardens with many elegant figures, among them the Prince of Wales. In Christie's auction of July 1945, the watercolour was sold for £2,730. When it reappeared at auction in 1967 the bidding ended at £11,000. During those twenty-two years, the owner was not only seeing and enjoying this masterpiece but was, in a sense, being paid over a pound a day for doing so!

Before the war, in the mid-1930s, my father bought a fine flower painting by Roelandt Savery (1576-1639) for £80 from a Dutch collector. He later sold it to a private collector in England, after cleaning and re-framing, for £120. At Sotheby's on 24 March 1965, the same little picture measuring $9\frac{1}{4} \times 7$ inches, was sold for £8,000. A distinguished client of our firm can recall his family selling a remarkable Rembrandt for £10,000 before the First World War, which was auctioned at Parke-Bernet in New York in 1961 for £821,428.

The authority quoted in reference to any discussion of the history of prices is Gerald Reitlinger's book, *The Economics of Taste: The Rise and Fall of Picture Prices 1760-1960* (Barrie & Rockliff, 1961). Fascinating as this survey of two hundred years can be, the eight years from Reitlinger's concluding date 1960 can be equally interesting and perhaps more instructive. What has happened in these years has made some of his summaries quaintly out of date.[1] For example, when discussing the varying popularity of Rembrandt in the past, he concludes that Rembrandt was universally popular in the first thirty years of the present century, but this position has not been maintained since! Yet, within five years, Aristotle and Homer at New York (November 1961) already referred to, and the portrait of Titus at Christie's (March 1965) were to fetch over £750,000

[1] This was inevitable, and I intend no criticism of this splendid book.

each, and other far less important examples over £100,000.[1] I am reminded of the reply, made many years ago by an art dealer to his client, who had ventured the opinion that a painting could not be worth that sum of money: 'On the contrary, it's the pictures which give the money its value!'

If it appears unrealistic to quote Rembrandt prices, they are symptomatic of the general trend which may be paralleled in the work of lesser figures. In 1966, an exceptionally good Ibbetson watercolour entitled 'Summer in St James' Park', with topographical interest and many elegant figures, was sold at Sotheby's for £2,700. The quality of the pair of Ibbetson watercolours illustrated in the last chapter was comparable with this drawing in every respect. But assuming, harshly, that the pair together were only a third as valuable as the single, larger drawing, the pair would be worth £900. In 1957 they were bought at Sotheby's for £160, the pair. In the same way, an important Rowlandson drawing, 11×15 inches, of a hunting scene with many fine figures, horses and hounds, was sold in November 1960 for £400 at Sotheby's. In 1967 a drawing of the same size entitled 'The Duel', a good drawing but not nearly so good nor so interesting in content, fetched £1,000. On this basis, the 1960 drawing would be worth at least a minimum of £1,500-£2,000. The same parallels can be drawn in marines and most other fields.[2] If this were not so, the price ranges mentioned would be very different. What is more important than comparisons and statistics are the lessons to be learnt.

Most of the striking comparisons of the kind cited are concerned with paintings and drawings which, in their

[1] I am thinking particularly of two paintings sold at Sotheby's in 1964, 'An Apostle Reading', of 1661, £168,000 and a 'Still Life of Partridges', £110,000.

[2] See *The Times*, Sotheby Index on English Painting which is to be published in 1968. Impressionists, Old Master prints and silver have already been covered.

different ways represent the best of the artist's work. The best examples usually move up in value much more rapidly than a good but average work. Thus, they can be misleading as to the appreciation of the artist's work as a whole. In other words one is back to the same basic principle that everything depends on the individual painting and there are no general rules. However spectacular some of the figures, they do not mean that paintings are automatically going up in value. It bears repeating that if pictures fail to come up to the mark, in terms of authenticity, condition, and quality, they may not be a good investment at all.

The expression used to describe paintings and drawings which answer well in each of these three respects, is that they are of museum quality. In other words, they are acceptable in every way to a body of experts for permanent acquisition – no matter whether it is a Rembrandt or an English watercolour. Museums belong to no particular corner of the world, and good paintings are now often of international, rather than merely national, importance.

The growth in the number of museums and other permanent collections, and the force of their purchasing power, has brought some pressure to bear on the activities of the private collector. In the face of diminishing opportunities, the sooner you can begin your collecting the better. I realize that cries of scarcity have been raised since the beginning of the century, but at the present time they are real and not founded on trends or changeable fashions. In recent years, it has been forecast that the capital gains tax and the credit squeeze, and the general economic depression, would deter buyers and reduce prices. In the event, the opposite has happened and there have been record turnovers in the salerooms and in the art business in general. Devaluation has now given a further impetus to these developments. It is therefore very understandable that prices should have risen and no reason whatever why they should not continue to do so. If, as I have said, you enter the field anew, you will think in present-day and future values and not in the past. There is still wide scope for the new collector and the investment value of good paintings wisely bought, is unshakeable.

Paintings must have a sound potential for the future, but essentially exist as background assets and not financial speculations. In this way, you will be a true collector.

The Care of Paintings

The preservation and restoration of paintings is a task for experts alone. I have seen it stated in books purporting to guide the collector, that it is in some respects a do-it-yourself job. Let me emphasize that apart from dusting a painting and its frame carefully, and cleaning the glass of a watercolour, you should always leave anything further to a properly qualified person. I should, in parenthesis, say that you may well be able to do the hanging and lighting of a picture yourself, but it would not be amiss especially in respect of the lighting, which I consider very important, to have expert advice. What restorers dread most of all is not a painting which has a hole in it, as so many laymen think, but a painting which has been over-cleaned. Whether one calls it a picture which has been thinned or skinned, as some people do, an over-cleaned picture is the most difficult to restore and the one to which the most harm has been done. By harm is meant deterioration in its value artistically and financially. Much of the damage of this kind encountered by restorers has been done by well-intentioned but foolish people seeking to avoid the cost of professional work, and in doing so, reduce the value of the painting by many times that amount. If your paintings are in good condition at the outset and professionally maintained, you need have no worries as to their durability. What the owner can do for his paintings is to see that they are comprehensively insured against theft, destruction by fire and flood, and accidental damage.

My final word would be to wish you good fortune in your collecting, and to suggest that by bringing up your children in a home with fine paintings, you will give them a gift of appreciation which can neither be bought nor recaptured once it is missed.

Index

Note Numbers in bold figures refer to illustration numbers, not page numbers. Bracketed figures refer to footnotes.

Anderson, William, 82–4, 85, **3**
animal and sporting paintings, 45, 58, 106
Apollo, 54
apprenticeship, 18
aquatint, 86, 101 (2)
'Art and Architecture' books, 52 (2)
Art Prices Current, 70
Arts Council exhibitions, 44 (1), 45
Arts Review, 54

Barret, George, Senior, 44 (3)
beach scenes, 114
Becher, Captain Edward, 108
Benezit, E., *Dictionnaire,* 51 (1)
Bernt, Walther, 52–3
bitumen, 29
Blommers, Bernardus-Johannes, 114, **43**
books, art, 47–53, 105
Boucher, François, 44
Boudin, Eugène, 114
British Museum, 41
Brooking, Charles, 45 (2), 98
brushwork, 17–18, 19, 21
Bryan, *Dictionary of Painters,* 51
Bührle, Emil, 44 (1)

Cabane, Pierre, 44 (1)
Canaletto, Antonio, 33–4, 53, 88
canvas, 2–9; stretching, 4–6; lining, 6–8
Carmichael, James Wilson, 111–12, **38, 39**
catalogues; exhibition, 45, 53, 64
saleroom, 60–1, 62–3
Victoria and Albert, 40
Chambers, George, 109, **35**
Christie's, 5–6, 45 (2), 56–60, 102, 118
Clark, Sir Kenneth, 47–8, 89 (2)
Clay, Rotha Mary, 93 (2), 99
Cleveley, John, Junior, 84–5, **4**
Clifford, Derek, 105
cobalt blue, 30
colourmen, artists', 31
colours, 26 (1), 29–30, 35–7
'fugitive', 28–9, 75–6
condition, 8, 64, 65–6, 120, 121
of watercolours, 75–6
Connoisseur, The, 54, 88 (1), 90 (2)
Constable, John, 18, 37, 41–2, 104–5, **31**
Constable, W. G., 37, 53 (2), 92 (1), 97 (1)
copying, 25–6, 61–2
Corot, Jean Baptiste, 62, 112, 113
Cotman, John Sell, 105, **30**
Courant, Maurice, 113–14, **46**
Cozens, J. R., 40

cracking (*craquelure*), 23–5, 26
cradling, 14
Cuyp, Aelbert, 10–11, 50, 61, 106

Davies, Randall, 85 (1), 108 (1)
dealers, 66–72
Delacroix, Eugène, 49–50
details, 24, 47–8
direct painting, 35
Downman, John, 106–7, **34**
drawing, preliminary, 21, 74–5
Dutch Art and Architecture, 52
Dutch school, *17C.,* 9–10, 11–12, 12–13, 60, 61, 115–16
Duveen, Joseph, 106

encyclopaedias, 51–2
exhibitions, special, 43–5

Farington, Joseph, 92–3, **14**
Fernandi, Francesco (Imperiali), 114–15, **41**
Flemish painting; *14–15C.,* 9–10 *17C.,* 12–13, 115
flower, painting, *17C.,* 35, 115–16
forgery, 5, 25, 62
Fragonard, Jean-Honoré, 53 (1)
French *18C.* painting, 11, 44; *19C., see* Impressionists
fresco, 17

Gainsborough, Thomas, 61, 98–9, 103; portraits, 26–7, 28
galleries; dealers', 67–8, 71–2
public, xvii, 38–47, 120; *see also* names of
Gérôme, Jean-Léon, 113, **44, 45**
Gilpin, Sawrey, 44–5
Gilpin, William, 44
Girtin, Thomas, 45 (1), 105
glazing, 21–2
Gombrich, Prof., 50, 51
gouache, 74 (2), 102–3, 115–16

Grant, Col. M. H., 52, 82 (3,) 86 (3), 87 (2), 89 (2), 91, 98
Griffith, Moses, 95, **17**
Grimm, Samuel Hieronymous, 93–4, **15**
Guardi, Francesco, 34

Hals, Frans, 5, 37
handling, 17–18, 19
hanging, 121; on approval, 69
watercolours, 77–8
Hardie, Martin, 76, 77, 82 (3), 84 (1), 85 (1), 87 (2), 93, 93 (2), 94, 95 (1), 96, 97
Harpignies, Henri-Joseph, 112–13, **42**
Harrods, 58
Historic Houses and Castles, 43
Holland, James, 108–9, **36**

Ibbetson, Julius Caesar, 24, 96, 99–101, 103, 119, **2, 22, 23, 24**
impasto, 7, 22
Impressionists, French, 35–7, 44 (1)
investment, xiv–v, 72, 121
Italian painting, 4, 9

Jones, Thomas, 92, **13**
Jongkind, Johann, 114

Kenwood, exhibitions at, 44–5, 89
Iveagh Bequest, 11 (1), 24 (4)
Kneller, Sir Godfrey, 30

La Cave, Peter, 96, **18**
landscapes; *18C.,* 89–106; *19C.,* 108–12
Laurie, A. P., 5
Lawrence, Sir Thomas, 30, 48
Lemaître, Henri, 77
lighting of picture, 121
lining a picture, 6–8
Long, Basil S., 94 (1)
Lorraine, Claude, 50, 90
Lugt, Frits, 5 (1)
Luny, Thomas, 86–7, **9**

magazines, 53–4
Manet, Edouard, 37
marine painting, 81–8; *19C.*, 108–12
marks, on supports, 5–6, 11
Marlow, William, 34, 88, 103–4
'Masters' series, 48–9
maulsticks, 24–5
Monet, Claude, 36
Morland, George, 100
Moses, Henry, 86, **6, 7**
mounting watercolours, 78
Murray, Peter and Linda, 50–1
museum quality, 120
museums, 38–47, 120; *see also* names,
  lectures and publications, 46
  local, 22, 42–3, 44
Museums and Galleries, 43

nails, 3, 5
National Gallery, 22, 25, 31–2, 33, 34, 46, 63–4
National Maritime Museum, 82
National Portrait Gallery, 22, 23, 26–7, 30–1
Nicholson, Francis, 96–7, **19, 20**
Norwich School, 43, 61, 105

oil painting, 20–2, 37; ageing of, 28–9
Old Water Colour Society, 97,
  Journal, 108 (1)
Oppé, Paul, 101 (3)

paints, 19–22, 37, 74
panel, wood, 9–17
paper, 74, 75; millboard, 112
Parke-Bernet Inc., New York, 56, 118
pastel, 107
Paul Mellon Foundation, 52
Payne, William, 94–5, **16**
Pennant, Thomas, 95
pentimenti, 29
Perroneau, Jean Baptiste, 107
Pocock, Nicholas, 85–6, **5**
Pointillism, 36
portraits, 3–4, 21, 23, 24, 26–7, 28–9, 30, 31, 106–8
pot-boilers, 65
preservation, 13–15, 76, 121–2
price, 69–71, 80–1, 89; *see also* value
priming, 11, 12, 16–17, 21
provenance, 18, 63
pupil assistants, 19
Pyne, James Baker, 109–10, **37**

Reitlinger, Gerald, 118
Rembrandt, 19, 24, 50, 59 (1), 118–19
Renoir, Auguste, 109
reproductions; aquatint, 86
  copies, 25–6, 61–2
  postcard, 47
restoration, 8, 13–14, 15, 65–6, 121;
  of watercolours, 76
Reynolds, Grahame, 76–7
Reynolds, Sir Joshua, 29, 31, 48, 85, 94
  portrait by, 23, 24, 27
Roberts, David, 110–11, **40**
Roberts, Keith, 48
Robinson, Michael, 82 (1)
Rosa, Salvator, 103
Rowlandson, Thomas, 104, 118, 119, **28**
Royal Academy, 44, 83, 96 (1), 100, 101, 105, 107; Diploma Gallery, 45
Rubens, Peter Paul, 31–3, 49, 50
Ruisdael, Jacob, 90
Russell, John, 107–8, **32**

salerooms, 56–66; *see also* names
Sandby, Paul, 77, 84, 94, 99, 101–3, **25, 26, 27**
Sandby, William, 101 (1)
Savery, Roelandt, 118
'school pictures', 62
Scott, Samuel, 34, 88, 103–4
Serres, Dominic, 87, 98, **21**
Serres, John Thomas, 87–8, 98, **8**

Seurat, Georges, 36
Shee, Martin Archer, 108, **33**
signature, the artist's, 25, 61, 79
Smith, George, 89–92, **10, 11, 12**
Smith, John, 90, 91, **11**
Sorenson, Cyril, 45
Sotheby's, 45 (2), 56–7, 59–60, 118, 119
  Times Index, 114 (1), 119 (2)
Spanish painting, 4
spotting, 76
sporting paintings, 106
still-life painting, 35, 115
Storck, Abraham, 24, **1**
stretchers, 4–6; keys, 4, 7
Stubbs, George, 58
support, 2–17
  canvas, 2–8; panels, 9–17

technique, 17–22; examples, 23–30, 31–5 *19C.*, 30–1, 35–7
temperature, 13, 14
Thieme-Becker, *Dictionary*, 51
Towne, Charles, 105–6, **29**
transferring, 15
Turner, Joseph Mallord William, 37, 61, 75 (1), 105

under-painting, 21, 28–9

valuation, 70
value of pictures, xiv, xvi, xvii, 117–21; *see also* price
Van de Velde, Willem, 82
Van Der Neer, Aert, 11
Van Gogh, Vincent, 50
Van Goyen, Jan, 12, 15, 53, 60, 79
Van Os, Jan, 57
Velasquez, Diego, 37
Venice, 33–4, 109
Victoria and Albert Museum, 18, 40–1, 76–7, 112; Library, 51, 110

Wallace Collection, 44
Ward, James, 100
Warner, Oliver, 86 (1)
warping, 13–14
watercolours; paints, 20, 74; condition, 76, 79–80; displaying, 77–8; in museums, 40–2, 44; books on, 76–7
  English, 73–81; examples, 81–106
  19C., 79, 108–12
Waterhouse, Prof., 52, 114 (3)
Watts, F. W., 42
Wildenstein, Georges, 53 (1)
Williams, Iolo, 77, 95 (1)
Wilson, Arnold, 86 (2), (3)
Wilson, Peter, 56, 57
Wilson, Richard, 43, 50, 92, 98, 104
Windsor, 34 (1), 101 (3)
Withoos, Mathias, 115–16
Withoos, Pieter, 115–16, **47, 48**
wood, *see* panels
worms, 14
Wright, Joseph, 42, 89, 103–4